WHEN THE VIRGIN FALLS

Nigel Clayton

I0170813

Published in Australia by Nigel Clayton in 2012

Printed by CreateSpace, an Amazon.com Company.

Nigel Clayton, 1963
When the Virgin Falls, Second Edition.
ISBN 978-0-9806585-9-0

WHEN THE VIRGIN FALLS

Other Titles by this Author

The Long Road to Rwanda
Colonies of Earth
Fall of the Inca Empire
Inca Myths and Way of Life
The Templar: and the City of God
The Templar: and the Temple of Káros
The Templar: and the Cross of Christ
Underworld
Spacescape
Space Opera – Heaven and Hell
Tom of Twofold Bay
The Zuytdorp Survivors
Afghan
Afghan: The Script
Chivalry
The Caves of Hiroshima
Scourge
The Cure
Amazon
Furious George
This Pestilence, Bergen-Belsen
Templar, Assassination, Trial & Torture
Underworld
Dreamtime - An Aboriginal Odyssey
Kibeho: Original Script
The Kibeho Massacre: As It Happened
Non, Je Ne Regrette Rien - No, I (We) Have No Regrets
The Matter with Karen Mitchell

About the Author

Nigel joined the Australian Army in 1980 at age 17yrs and 2 months, and after completing training at Kapooka was whisked away to the School of Infantry, Singleton, New South Wales, Australia.

He served in the Infantry until injury forced a medical discharge upon him in 1996, after having served in Southeast Asia, 1982; PNG (with the AATPT), in 1990: during the Bougainville Crisis; and in Rwanda, 1995: known world-wide for the Kibeho Massacre which occurred on April 22nd of that year.

Serving in PNG was a major highlight within his career.

He was married in 1999 and has two children.

WHEN THE VIRGIN FALLS

GENERAL INFO

The term 'British Expeditionary Force' was used to refer to us, the forces present in France prior to the end of the First Battle of Ypres on 22 November 1914, or Wipers as coequally accepted by us all, for to get your tongue around some of the French names was more than a chore. By the end of 1914 we had, for a better word, been wiped out, although we did manage to stop the German advance. But maybe for morale, custom, or simple courtesy of our sacrifice B.E.F. continued to remain the official name of the British Army in France and Flanders until the end of the First World War.

The German Emperor, Kaiser Wilhelm, was rather dismissive of our band-of-brothers and although I know today, it being created for propaganda purposes, was reported to have stated: 'Exterminate those treacherous English and walk over General French's contemptible little army'.

Britain declared war on Germany on the fourth day of August in 1914 and within five days the BEF had commenced its deployment, being the best trained and most experienced for we were volunteers and regulars to a man, whereby a vast majority of the French and German armies were conscripts and had little regular formation to speak of in regard to our percentages. We were initially 80,000 strong; the French and Germans holding over 1 million apiece; but numbers would change drastically over the coming years.

The first British contact with the Germans was on the 21st August, 1914, when a reconnaissance team upon bicycles ran into the enemy near a place called Obourg. It was here that the first British casualty was awarded the Germans. It was the following day that I, as a member of the 2nd Battalion, Royal Dublin Fusiliers, landed upon French soil at a place called Boulogne, where others before us had landed at Le Havre. What happened next was four years of utter devastation and misery, far from the adventure that many sought, and far from being over-by-Christmas, but for those that were home by Christmas… they were in a poor condition in most cases, suffering for the remainder of their pitiful lives, some with two legs and a right arm missing: what a state to be in.

Oh, and one more thing to tell which is hard to admit but very, very true. My wife fell pregnant whilst we were out of wedlock but I suppose in the years to come this became more unimportant with social acceptance and understanding. I shall also tell you something else, unbelievable though it may sound, and that is that my wife was in labour and gave birth to a healthy boy on the 21st August, and here I am on the 22nd, setting foot upon foreign soil and not yet having seen the babies face. All I could hope for was that I would be alive to see them both in the not-so-distant future, but how were we to know the extent of that before us all?

This is my story and I am Denis Patrick Kelly.

WHEN THE VIRGIN FALLS

22nd AUGUST 1914

I say this not to make men look like fools but to allow the world to reflect on just a minute example of patriotism and chivalry for the old world was far behind us, but there was a place in many hearts where the war did appeal to men of solid idealism. It turned out to be a dangerous thing but also a necessary evil for without the efforts of all those that raced against the bullets of the German machine guns there would be no victory and possibly no England to speak of; but for many that joined it was to be their adventure of a lifetime and was seen as their duty to king and country.

Many a time I sat by a warm and cosy fire to listen upon stories of old men having fought against the Zulu at places like Isandlwana and Rorke's Drift, or the battles of the Boar War, for there was no such thing as television back in the days of glory where one's own fortitude was his good nature and words such as a-trustworthy-Hun were never heard, and cowardice was so seldom seen that I imagined it to be a word made up to aid in the mustering of courage when the shells came tumbling down around you: despite the fact that courage was always in a mustered state.

There were others, too, that joined for oblique reasons; is that the right word? If not then it's a polite one, for some were pressured to join by family, friends, and co-workers, conned and coerced into signing up as beer was poured down their throats: for want of Dutch courage some men need… a sprinkle of bravado [but they were never cowards]. For some it was a simple matter of being a family tradition.

My first taste of battle wasn't the fields' of Mons, however, but the ground between it and Paris. It wasn't so much a direct conflict but being fired upon by heavy guns was part and parcel of battle to me: now that I look upon it as I sit upon my favourite chair wrapped in aging skin some 50-odd years after those horrid days. It would be a far stride though for one to take without hearing of the battle which was to set us in motion. It was as though my teenage years were knocking at the door for the stories to be voiced; for a voiced, visual representation to be provided.

The Battle of Mons may not be considered by many as a battle but more a withdrawal. I like to look at it as a subsidiary movement of the Battle of the Frontiers, for withdrawal can sound like such a cowardly brand unless employed with the word 'tactical' placed before it.

This is how it came about.

Being a member of the 2nd Royal Dublin Fusiliers we were hard at work getting on with closing the gap upon the front when our brothers sat in position on the left of the French, meaning that the men of the BEF were required to hold the line of the Mons-Condé Canal against a numerically superior enemy from encircling them: those evil sods of Europe, the German First Army. It was the spoken word that we were outnumbered six to one and from the stories I heard during our long march westward I can believe it.

The 2nd Dublin was of the 4th Division, 10th Brigade. We had marched through the port and streets to be given a hero's welcome by the citizens of Boulogne, flags flying, children waving, a band playing our favourite tunes as we made our way forward. But the fanfare didn't last long for we were out of there rather quickly and soon could hear the guns firing as we advanced, when at the halt and awaiting further development, or moving forward. The noise of the crowd behind us simmered and the grinding of our boots upon the road momentarily paused. The front was still a long way away but the sound of artillery firing could be heard. But the sound of artillery was nothing compared to what it would be on the morrow.

We hadn't known it at the time but the first action had already taken place at 0600hrs this morning when a patrol made up of men from the 4th Dragoon Guards to the northeast of Mons fell upon a small band of German cavalry at Casteau. Full of vigour and willing to get the job done the guards gave chase and it wasn't until the horses were getting used to the pace of the chase that the Germans turned and fired upon the pursuers.

As the noise of the guns in the distance came upon our ears I considered by position amongst the throng. Here we were, dressed in khaki, webbing pressed around our waists and pack upon our backs, over 61 pounds of equipment weighing us down for not a soul amongst us had yet seen good reason to lessen the load, but the near future would see that changed in a hurry. And in my palm I cradled my Lee-Enfield rifle, a most remarkable weapon indeed, so much so that it was contestably sought after by the Canadians: when they arrived. It was a bolt-action and magazine fed and any soldier of his majesty's BEF was able to fire between 20 and 30 aimed shots per minute. And although the Canadians are not yet here I must advise you accordingly, before I forget, of their Ross rifle. What a shambles it was and many stories surround it, but more on those a little later. As for now I must tell you that those poor bastards, the Canadians, had a hell of a time fighting the war with the Ross, for it was a longer weapon and not so steady in the hand, its weight only preceding its inability. The bayonet often fell off the weapon and keeping it clean was a chore and a half. We can thank the good lord that we Britons had the Lee Enfield. The Ross was accurate enough but utterly useless at rapid firing where constant jamming was the normal occurrence. It was simply atrocious and had little to no ability when trying to ward off a hoard of sods coming towards you with anger scribed upon their faces and steam pouring from their ears ready to disembowel you with glimmering bayonets of their own. Rapid fire over more than two minutes or more would see it overheat and throw in the towel for the bolt of the weapon could not be unlocked unless hit with the bayonet and kicked back with the heel of your boot: you don't believe me; then you have plenty more to read of this and plenty to learn and maybe then you will accept it all as true.

But back to the story at hand.

And as we made way towards the front the men at Mons welcomed the night with entrenching tools being readied. It was here that Sir John French, commander of the BEF, was to hold the line cast before him: the Mons-Condé Canal. Out with entrenching tools and dig, dig, dig was the order passed around. All along the canal the men put down their positions in order to hold the line, four infantry divisions and five brigades of cavalry, some history books will say a total of almost 80,000 men but I shall tell you different, and although I have no proof of numbers I do have good hearing and sense, and when a man tells me stories of conflict and strategy unfolded I take note, for Sir Horace Lockwood Smith-Dorrien was here, our Corps commander, watching over the 3rd and 5th Divisions with pride, but we were yet to show our face as we made our way to the front to consolidate our 4th Division with the remainder of the II Corps under Smith-Dorian, and there were others at our back: should these men yet count in their numbers? But they were seemingly in good hands, had good support with 54 18-pounders, four 60-pounders and 18 4.5 inch howitzers. But those damn sods, the Hun, had outdone us for the artillery support on their side was far superior in number when compared to our own.

23rd AUGUST 1914

It was on the morning of the 23rd that the Battle of Mons took place and as usual it was the dawning of the day which welcomed the fall of artillery shells from the sky, a bombardment upon the British lines so fierce that those so new to battle almost soiled their pants through sheer terror, but they held together like all good men do when faced with great adversity.

It wasn't until 0900hrs that the German infantry opened with their initial assaults upon the British line, and it was to be their undoing, a lesson to be learnt for all time, and an ironic beginning to German manufacture that was to see many men killed on the fields of glory; why? Because great emphasis had been placed upon every soldier in the British Army to such a degree that we could kill a man at 300 yards without so much as one miss in twenty and were able to pour out such a mass of rapid fire, being

20-30 rounds [and whether or not you prefer the term, cartridge/bullet, is up to you] per minute, per man, that the whole German First Army thought they were up against a military organization so well equipped with machine guns that they immediately set about organizing their factories to cough up machine guns of their own. This of course helped create the great massacre known as the Somme two years later: I am sure of this, but there was more than a single factor in the miseries we were all to face during the Somme Offensive.

The sods' assault upon the four bridges spanning the canal, four battalions alone pressed upon the Nimy Bridge. Here the ground was defended by the 4th Battalion of the Royal Fusiliers.

The men's great marksmanship skills and solid wall of fire worked wonders this day; possibly too well. It was legendary marksmanship skills now confronting the sod which saw them cower here and there but for the most part they came upon the front line spurred on by men at their rear with orders to shoot any retiring conscript.

But the initial assault was not as thick and fast as what it was to become.

It was becoming quite clear; the German sods were attempting a right hook upon the line held by the BEF and the French Fifth Army to entrap the allies and bring them into ill-repute, looking for a quick victory on this the Franco-Belgian and Franco-German borders.

Hold the left of the British line, Sir Horse – with all due respect – Smith-Dorrien, for the Germans are about to unleash hell upon the II Corps and this would eventuate in what was to become a major British withdrawal. The BEF was about to meet their adversary for the German First Army was made up of 18,000 men, or as one intellectual from Company headquarters had said, ten men for every three feet of ground for each mile of frontage, and our 80,000 [less those on the approach] were not in one place at the same time but spread over a vast area.

I'll be damned. It was well that we were all here of our own choosing and not conscripts, and I don't say this to give a pat-on-the-back to all those involved, for past heroics of services rendered to country cannot be forgotten, but the British Army of 1914 was the finest force that ever departed her soil for war. We also had experience on our side like none other for there were many 'old sweats' amongst us, soldiers who had come under fire in South Africa during the Boer War, and I'm sure I saw a face the other day which spoke words of Zulu conflict and killings against the marauding impi. There was nothing like a consoling word or two from and old sweat to a young regular; a veteran giving good advice and morale support to a young man who had yet to spill blood.

I could feel the blood spurting through my veins as we made our way towards the war; I could feel the blood causing through my veins as stories unfolded before me during the nights of the withdrawal from Mons. It seemed to me that the valour of those at Rorke's Drift was being witnessed once more at Mons and legendary status was once again being born unto the world. Having heard stories in pubs over the years I reflected upon what would come of this war and its battles yet unborn. Would we be spoken of so fondly; would it be our turn in the future to have stories told of our victories and sunken defeats?

Our men on the front line could not honestly believe their ears and eyes in most cases and again you might find this hard to believe but the sods were advancing thick as you please, and in some places they had their arms linked and were singing songs. What was it that the Generals had told their men? It seemed as though they were off to a party, but our blokes took good care to teach them a lesson or two.

So many young men, conscripts one and all, advancing to their death, or to be maimed, irreparable. It would come to pass that men like General Haig, with or without his promotion to Field Marshal, was branded a warmonger with no regard at all for the safety of his men, nor the lives that they gave so gallantly, but the enemy officers that looked down upon the rank and file of Germany's front line soldier was beyond belief. There was a complete and utter disregard for human life. Compared to this we had hope on our side and with hope there was possible salvation, for we still did not know the full consequences to come of this war in Europe.

Our Generals would come under great scrutiny from historians and ourselves, as men who lead a million lambs to their slaughter, but they were experienced and had been taught great lessons during the two Boar wars of years past. It was here that a landmark change was inducted, in the way in which soldiers advanced their line of attack towards the enemy by conducting a series of rushes within the extended order; known as a ten wave attack. You will be utterly shattered by the stories I will tell you soon enough. It was a method of attack pursued to see to it that large numbers of men would not come under fire at the same time: so why was it not used more often; why in hells name were we to see so little of this method?

But even though they were conscripts they did have a brain and the men ordering forward the all-encompassing attack of the private soldier and NCOs, officers dotted here and there, were quick to learn their lesson. Attacking in close order was not to work and so open formation was quickly employed. The initial repulse of the German attack was now to change; their heavy losses would now be given a much sought after reprieve.

The Britons were now to take more care in their delivery of rapid fire and the trigger finger of each master hand was given a little rest, back to 15 well aimed shots per minute, which was closer to the required standard as given at Aldershot during training. It was now that the Second Division lining up along Sambre Canal took more heed of their instructors.

Firing a high volume of fire into a mass of infantry so dense that there was hardly room to breathe allowed for quick and easy kills and wounded to be attained, but where the density was more lax so the numbers in KIA and WIA diminished. Deliberately, well-aimed shots might well have slowed the process of the bullets flying down range but the ability to concentrate all the more on the centre of the seen mass allowed for more KIA rather than WIA. This may or may not have been a better option, even though the situation called for it, for a WIA held up many enemy as they needed to see to the withdrawal of the wounded: hence our orders in the near future, at such places like the Somme, changed for what I would call 'the worse', where we received orders NOT to attend the wounded and to leave them where they lay in order to continue with the advance.

The initial attacks were waved aside as though nothing to be concerned with, for if the sods wanted to die so quickly then the BEF could accommodate, but now they came again at 1100hrs. But here and there the Germans presented themselves as massed infantry, advancing in column almost as before. To wish them a little closer would assure a quick victory, but some things cannot be granted.

But let me tell you more of the Lee-Enfield rifle. It was rather effective to 600 yards and a well-trained man was hardly met with a problem in mustering enough skill to drop a target at that range. In the initial phases of war men needed to grapple with the noise of war that surrounded them but it didn't take long for this to be, more or less, ignored and good marksmanship skills to come of maturity. Although the magazine held ten rounds of .303 ammunition the clips which fed the magazine held five. 15 well aimed shots per minute was the required standard, more than this was often seen and rewarded with a cheery smile and a pat on the back.

Although I spoke of numbers in regards to our men against theirs, the situation wasn't rosy. Those at the points of attack were grossly outnumbered and the defence of the crossings at the canal became unbelievably hard going, each man fighting hard to control his fire from hastily dug positions which in most cases was little more than a shallow scrape in the ground.

The Royal Fusiliers did all they could to hold their ground and were tested to the full, and to the right of them was the Middlesex Regiment and the Gordon Highlanders: the Royal West Kent Regiment and the King's Own Scottish Borderers also fell victim to the misgivings of war and suffered horribly. Casualties were so high amongst these units that the divisional reserve, the Royal

Irish Regiment, were called upon to bolster the defence along with effective artillery support. With this move the BEF managed to hold the bridges and repulse the sodding advance of the Hun.

The machine gun was tenacious but the remarkable exploits of a German private, swimming across the canal, saw the swing bridge machinery operated and German attack enhanced. By 1500hrs an order to retire [tactically] was received and as the sun said its good night a new line of defence was formed allowing the sods to build pontoon bridges to aid in the crossing of the canal for the bridges would not suffice: there number was so great.

Soon after a most unpleasant message had reached the ears of our good men; the French were retreating, which put the British right flank at jeopardy of being overrun and defeated.

The situation was remarkably unstable. The forward most positions were abandoned and some close fighting was associated with the movement from one position to another as soldiers fell back. So vicious was it that some of our own were taken as prisoner but not before dismantling the machines guns we had and throwing the parts into the canal to prevent the sod from employing them against the BEF.

24th AUGUST 1914

The retreat had been ordered at 0200hrs and such a tactical move saw battalions and regiments of men, horses and artillery, pack their packs, saddle bags and wagons for a move towards the southwest and Paris, though no one in their right mind considered that the withdrawal would take the BEF that far.

Many rear-guard actions were called for as the rearmost elements undertook a fighting withdrawal, buying the much needed time for those at the lead to get away relatively unscathed from further damage.

The sod didn't let up for a minute and the follow up continued without a break until the village streets behind the fighting at the canal were a place of mayhem and immoral activity. The sod were suffering as heavily as us in regards to casualties, be they KIA,

9

WIA, missing or taken prisoner. Many times did the men of the BEF see to it that the Germans payed dearly for the ground they gained by mowing them down with machine gun fire and in villages all around the Germans continued to advance in the wake of our withdrawal. In places we heard stories of the sod breaking into houses and taking citizens from their property under protest, to use them as human shields against the hostile BEF fire. Such was the way of the conscript and others like them.

The soldiers of the British Army withdrew down streets, taking periodic cover in doorways and behind garden walls, seemingly running further and further as ground was given away to the unstoppable advance.

Cavalry were forced to dismount in places but only due to their great courage in bringing heart-felt relief to those in the greatest need and at places where being outflanked was almost attained by the sod. And all day long it continued without a break; withdraw, withdraw, withdraw.

The French were continuing to retreat and so without a flank to support them the BEF needed to continue as well. The line in which we were to withdraw to was henceforth given up and further withdrawal planned hastily.

The withdrawal would last for two weeks and cover over 200 miles in distance: some say it was 180 miles, other say 250; all I can say is that the route wasn't exactly direct and to tell the truth I don't believe my feet gave a damn, for I was a ruined man by the end of it as was everyone else. It was along this route of movement that we men of the 2nd Royal Dublin Fusiliers were to come under control of our beloved Sir Horse; yes indeed, who I like to think as being a stallion of a leader. The move ever rearward was much the same as the battlefields we were to fight upon in the near future, a flat surface terrain dotted with copses, in particular around Flanders, and the undulated folds of earth looking like ripples of water upon a reasonably still lake. Yes indeed, the ground on which we trop was very dull and would have remained that way if not for the beatings we endured both physically and mentally, and little chance did I take to actually approve, or otherwise, of the scenery.

And what in God's name were we, the 2nd, doing? We were transported by train in rather a hurry to a quaint enough village called Le Cateau [after an embarrassment with being disembarked at the wrong place and being forced to march as quick-as-you-please] and here we remained, preparing positions for what was to come: the Battle of Le Cateau.

It was a hot day, more so than most of us were used to, but war was hell.

By 1700hrs we were making much progress in regards to scrapes and short fighting trenches and our minds could not help but wander off slightly to the sky above. Our lads were in aeroplanes high above fighting the Germans in the sky as the German pilots dropped bombs upon us, and bullets were being shot from the guns of the British to try and bring them down. On the ground the scenario was rather different than the spacious above. On the ground there were friendly troops in their thousands moving past us as well as artillery pieces, cavalry, and wagons galore. It seemed to me that the movement away from the firing line was rather… jam-packed – but such thoughts of jam on bread should be cast aside for the minute. It didn't seem to be well organised for their were stragglers all about, and it was very well hurried all along, more like a route than anything else: such a dirty word should not be used.

25th AUGUST 1914

Today was not much different than the day before. There was movement along the road by night but for most of the men busy with the withdrawal there was time to sleep and gather some rest amidst the shelling which could be heard further afield.

We didn't know it at the time but tomorrow would see our baptism of fire come about in great haste, but for the time all we could do was prepare our positions and watch periodically as the men continued past us. I don't mind telling you that I could see us on their tail soon enough, joining the others of the BEF in the withdrawal, our delay action little more than that.

Again it was a terrible day with the heat and dust doing no justice to parched throats as the infantry continued on foot whilst officers sat upon the backs of horses. Sometimes you would see the cavalry come past leading their horses along by the reigns: giving them a rest I suppose; but does a horse get sore feet?

We saw remnants of the French Army cause further congestion, broken down wagons getting in the way of battalions on the go. Limbered artillery rattling past and on one a wheel fell off and had to be repaired then and there.

I couldn't help consider what it was that these men had gone through at Mons. I took the opportunity during the day to converse with a few but it was not for me to sit idle for too long when hard work was to be carried out. You could see the forlorn look upon their hanging faces; not hanging in shame but hanging through sheer exhaustion. Sure, the 2nd had force-marched from train station to Le Cateau, but nothing quite like what these men had done before us, having marched on empty stomachs and after a pitched battle. They were so tired looking and seemed so confused by the entire ordeal of the continuing retreat. One man wished to know what we were doing by digging so hard, saying that the positions would be given up soon enough to the advancing Germans, but I needlessly pointed out that we needed to bring the advance to a halt for as long as possible in order for us all to get clean away. There was also a river in front of us, a natural obstacle. That should also afford some time to us all. But he moved along soon enough. And then as he stood he said something to me, a short story. He asked me if I knew of the Angels of Mons and I naturally enough replied no. he told me that during the withdrawal of the front line at Mons and the subsequent move through village, a soldier within the ranks bellowed as loud as you please for St George to come to their aid. This chorus of song was then sung by many, all requesting St George to come to their aid. And then from out of nowhere appeared thousands upon thousands of English Long Bowman launching arrows in their tens of thousands into the air. They cut down the German advance and helped the BEF get away as cleanly as they could.

The archers had saved the day for the BEF and it was to become a legend.

I suppose we all have to believe in something.

Later that night I saw a regiment of cavalry; Scottish Greys they were, setting down for a few hours kip in the early hours of the night as the day turned to dusk. Several hours later and they were off again, and I know not why. I knew that the I Corp had been helping to cover the second's retreat from the front; maybe now it was the seconds turn to reciprocate and cover them in the withdrawal.

26th AUGUST 1914

The 2nd RDF was a part of 10th Brigade, 4th Division, under General French: Sir Horse [and I should get myself out of the habit of calling him that] being above him. We were at Le Cateau and it was time for us to meet the grinder.

I hear once more men say that they were outnumbered 6 to 1 at Mons, possibly even more, and now on the back foot we were outnumbered 3 to 1. These figures alone did not stand well but could have been much worse if not for the bravery of the cavalry [disrupting the enemies progress] in putting themselves in harm's way by shielding us as best as possible so that the infantry could gain further distance from those sods rushing us from behind, providing what respite they could to the poor, underpaid bastards known as the infantry; life and limb for a shilling a day. It was here that I know many good Irish voices were lost of this world. The battalion in which I served was almost down to half, all thanks to this battle called Le Cateau, that which I shall explain shortly, but I don't wish you to tire of my story, of repeated attacks, deaths, bodies, artillery, and so on and so forth. I don't wish you to tire of this story for it must be read or you shall never understand that which should always be purged from existence, and only memory shall provide good reason to steer from such slaughter-houses as World War II.

Four days at war and we were almost wiped out, this BEF of ours. The French Army had itself lost 40,000 men over the past four days, 27,000 on the day in which the order to retreat from Mons was given. We were in a sorry state. Just a few days at war and the suffering expected was already far exceeded; what would the future bring? I had trained at Aldershot, conducted many route marches between Salisbury Plain and our camp on many occasions, but nothing like the past few days, and far more was to come.

As we prepared ourselves for battle at Le Cateau I couldn't help notice the men, who were at Mons, withdrawing past us, we few with entrenching tools and a few sandbags. It was not easy to see for the sun had not fully risen as yet. They marched past wearily and most with their heads down, tired as tired can be. An officer then appeared beside the road and ordered that all greatcoats be left behind for the added burden of weight was so horrific, everyone's feet being so sore; and then the impossible, but obvious, occurred before me. For exchange of greatcoat the men were given a further 80 rounds of .303 ammunition. These poor men, who I was soon to follow in misery, were losing comfort for ammunition. What must be, must be, and so I continued to dig and prepare my position as best I could and the men at the roadside picked themselves up and moved wearily on, no good food in the stomach to think of but something dry and intangible handed to them and they walked on, walk on with the war at their backs, a handful of ammunition, and on only two hours sleep from the night before. It appeared for all intents and purposes that the march to safer quarters had turned horribly sour and was now little more than a hobble in most cases.

It was sometime after that, that the sods arrived in number and commenced their assault upon us but our artillery gave them hell. Just several days before our boys of the BEF had gunned them down at the approach with rapid, single shots from the Lee Enfield, but today they were getting good medicine from the heavy guns. It must have been completely unexpected and the good news was the lack of artillery which they had themselves at hand, for their advance would have been so quick and seemingly swift that they had a hard time in keeping the supplies up with them.

We inflicted many casualties upon the sod but the vast majority were simply blown to bits by the artillery pieces and shrapnel rounds too, bursting here and there, sending scores upon scores of metal through the air and breaking upon the sodding attacks, ripping men apart. Blown apart, ripped apart; either way you look at it the artillery battle of the ages was here and now, only to be outdone in the years ahead by more of the same but in much vaster numbers.

So we hold the ground we have been assigned and do our duty as best we can with the Lee Enfield and entrenching tool. I hope that the bayonet will not have to be used for my stomach for killing other people has not quite grown accustomed to the idea of taking life, and taking it from a distance is by far preferred than taking it with the cold steel currently residing in the scabbard which knocks upon my buttocks.

By mid-afternoon the casualties are mounting considerably and it looks as though the retreat will be given sooner rather than later, and with the arrival of the French cavalry we are spurred on by orders and officers screaming over the noise of battle.

The cavalry shield works well in our favour, obstructing the advancements of the sod upon the left and right flank. The sod is coming full steam ahead, there seems to be no stopping them in their advance. I have to say this for them; they have nerves of steel: either that or many guards to their rear who threaten to shoot them dead if they should try to withdraw from the fight, for the Kaiser wouldn't give a damn for a conscript.

Later that night, when it is fairly young and with the heat of the day still lingering in the air, though much milder and dissipating fast, we continue with the 'tactical' withdrawal. Of 40,000 men fighting at Le Cateau we have lost 7,812 in all quarters: dead, missing, wounded, and prisoners, a few of the prisoners being left

15

behind on purpose for they had been blinded. We have suffered heavily in casualties ourselves but I later learn that there were entire battalions wiped from the face of the earth. It is hard to believe that the courage of men can be so easily replaced with corpses. And then it starts to rain.

I see many guns to our rear, the artillery men removing their breech blocks and sights, some taking the sights with them and destroying the other. It is a calculated initiative to deny the enemy. But they only leave their guns behind where we must leave our men, those still breathing, good men with air in their lungs, those who I have trained with for so long.

You might now understand how unfortunate it is that men should be left aside to fend for themselves as prisoners of war, to hope that the moral equity of the Germans was enough to secure their lives into the future, for wounded men and those no longer able to walk would have to contend with surrender, so it is here that we part good company and many men, unable to keep up for many and varied reasons, must shake hands, where time is allowed such show of comradeship, and the battalions continue on towards Paris.

You can only feel poorly for those left behind. To surrender to the enemy was a torment of many minds. Never did I wish to hear the words *hände hoch* [hands up], and would much prefer to hear a wounded German scream out *kamerad; lazaretto* [comrade; hospital]. It is easy to see why I would prefer to see the fear and desperation painted upon the sods' faces instead of our own, so to express any further the preference would be ignorant of your intelligence, dear reader.

So retreat we do when the time is ripe and we once again make quick time along the hard surface of the road to join with those poor bastards the refugee, walking astride their meagre possessions. There is a vast difference and story to tell upon their faces. Not three days ago and we were greeted with cheers and pats upon the back and today the grim look upon the French is one of sheer misery. Some must leave the old behind; some leave all their possessions, homes, cattle, goats, chickens, clothing, furniture, pianos and other instruments of great luxury and contentment; but photographs are saved where they can be saved, memories of a lifetime where easily ported and taken along for the long journey to safety as the sod wreaks havoc upon their homes and property. I have let them down; we have let them down. I feel disgrace and want to help them all but I can't, for that is an impossible task.

Torrents of rain then assault us throughout the night, joining the sod in the demented abuse upon us all, both soldier, civilian, and even horses alike. This is a journey with no end to misery.

Some men are luckier than others and carry Vaseline with them; where they attained such a prize is beyond me for no one would have left the cliffs of Dover behind with a retreat considered, so I should assume that the treasure itself was one given by a refugee. It then occurs to me that its use would make my feet worse, not better, so I am thankful of not trying it myself. And so the march continues towards Paris with a great weight upon our backs and minds. Our water runs very low and stomachs are empty of food but still we do all we must to keep ahead of the sod that snaps at our heels and dispatches groups of cavalry to gather information on our condition, predicament, and weaknesses; but there are few weaknesses found within the bravado held within our hearts as we deny the enemy all satisfaction.

I see fruit trees here and there, not far off to the side of the road, and several of our men are picking at the fruit. Better for them to eat than the sod, and as my mind drifts from the walk I stagger and trip to find my face buried in the hard road, hardly softened by the rain as it falls upon us. I am helped up immediately by friends who mean more to me than the friends of home for these are of the same heart and mind as me. We come to learn of comradeship, to share in everything that comes our way, the trenches in the years to come helping us bind in a common misery, but at present the misery is the road, the long march, and the little mud upon my face as it drains away in the falling torrents from above.

I never thought it possible to fall asleep whilst walking, but before we are given the order to pull up and rest for a few hours I have seen many men fall down, as I had, during the treacherous walk through the night.

We all halt and fall to the ground as though given mercy and within minutes the entire column for as far as the eye can see is sleeping, all except the cavalry who attend an urgent need to slow the enemy in their approach.

So I close my eyes and then someone yells out that the march is to continue immediately. I have no idea as yet that the blink of the eye was in fact three hours of slumber for it is impossible to tell the difference: it's as though no sleep has been granted at all.

Men scurry to their feet but some are hard at work opening their haversacks to the world and discarding their equipment, getting rid of all they think they don't need, relinquishing at a throw the weight of their hard drudgery ahead, but I consider the action and give quickly to the temptation, but keeping that which will keep me warm by night for I do not wish to be without a little warmth when the time comes, even at the sake of a few more blisters upon the blisters I already have, and so I place my overcoat back into my haversack. This discarding of equipment is of the greatest temptation to all of us and it is quite against the rules to be doing so, but officers and NCOs seem not to care as they too join in, and any disciplinary action is thrown to the wind and washed away. Some men see to giving their meagre possessions to those refugees that pass: I saw one little girl give an apple to man who had handed her his entrenching tool, but we all keep the things that matter the most which include our weapon and all ammunition. It is a beautiful gift that the girl has given for the refugees are hungrier than us. She will not be forgotten.

I do not know what time it is but I guess it to be after midnight, which in turn would make this day the 27th, but it doesn't really matter any. And then I hear some artillery, it's very close indeed. I think it's German but not entirely sure. I listen more purposely and yes, it is German, far off to the flank and obviously cutting up others in the retreat; poor, tired infantry like me who even now in the early days of the war are thinking of a nice warm bed to sleep in. Instead I have a sore body, from head to toe, and the soles of my feet are not worth talking of for I feel as though I have none, the soles having been ground down to bare flesh. But we must continue along and urgently for no one wishes to die like this. We all volunteered for this war but we are not fanatic and did not join in order to die. But if I am to be killed then I can only hope that it is fast, but not too quickly. I would like one last second to contemplate my family so that I may die with a smile upon my face. And what are my chances of living through this war. At the time I considered it to be rather minute at around twenty per cent; being wounded… four times as heavy, but no matter what happened I did not wish to be deaf or permanently incapacitated with both arms missing. I cared little for my legs and would gladly give them up, but I could not do without my arms, in particular my right.

27 AUGUST 1914

I have been told that the reason for our little slumber last night was due to the sod not making good advantage of the situation by following up on their assaults upon us, believing that we had been hit so hard that we resembled little to be concerned about. It was this error which brought the greatest fortune for we could use our time wisely and extend the distance between them and us, gaining what we would all soon learn to be a total of five days of good advantage, allowing the cavalry to conduct their rear-guard actions along with selected infantry elements that were relieved of contingency action during the days that followed for all to have a turn. As it turned out we, the second, were praised for what we had done at Le Cateau, for we had done more than was bargained for. We had gained time, we had hit the sod hard with artillery, we had, in effect, turned a ruse upon him without even realising that a ruse had been put into effect. But it had come at a great loss to man-power; but this was war and no one needed reminding of it.

I was later to learn in life that old Sir Horse had been criticized by Field Marshall French for the action at Le Cateau, French having preferred, or so it would seem, for us to have continued with the withdrawal. And where would we all be if that had happened, I ask you all? My wife was very thankful for what she'd heard of the Horse, thankful that I was alive and given five extra days of unmolested marching, in some cases to music given by refugees upon the wagons which rattled along the road on which we walked. Mixed in amongst us and along either side of the road are the refugees in their thousands pushing prams, wheelbarrows and carts filled to the brim with their possessions.

They had allowed the BEF to escape the clutches of the sod. Gratification must also be awarded the 2nd Royal Munster Fusiliers of the 1st Corps, with whom I would serve directly when transferred in the future to the 16th Irish Division. They were withdrawing upon a different line of approach to ours, and no prouder moment could there be. As the 1st Corps continued to increase their break from the enemy behind them to twelve miles or more the Munsters were hard at it, halting the sod dead in his tracks for fourteen hours around Ètreux, losing almost 80 per cent of all ranks and having been out-numbered six to one.

And so the miles fall away far behind us as we continue glumly along, aided by the comradeship of those around us, even in times like this when the energy to continue the march was leaving us for dead, the occasional joke and show of good humour spurred us on.

During the day the dust from the road seemed to swell up around us turning our khaki into a dirty grey; the dust was everywhere. We could not shave and so our beards turned grey, and I swear to God that the dust was weighing us down without remorse. Irritating it is to have the nose clogged up, continuously by that horrid dry snot and crustacean-like layer of dryness, but the dust in the throat made one so dry that it was a wonder we could continue as we did and on the little water made available whilst placing one foot in front of the other with little rest. If it were left to the men themselves then I am sure there would be much more rest and a little slumber but the sergeants wouldn't allow it and they whipped us on with kind words and harsh, playing good cop, bad cop, giving us reason to continue with the pace and further reason not to halt.

Again there was the poor wretched soul that could continue no more and would collapse out of line upon the ground as we marched. Exhausted beyond belief we would have no choice but to leave the poor men to be taken as a German prisoners of war, but there were sergeants within the BEF that wouldn't stand for it and performed miracle after miracle in driving the men ever onwards, getting them up from the ground and putting them back into gear.

Further on we tread, continuing with the retreat for many days, and rarely do we see any infantry setting up any form of defence to halt the sodding advance, for we have knowledge and with knowledge we shall take advantage, for the Germans are nowhere to be seen: even though several scouting parties of the sod on horseback can be viewed through binoculars from time to time.

I am then reminded of the man that not so long ago accepted an apple from a child as we passed a small orchard: food ever on the mind. There are apples upon the branches of trees, seldom seen now but many earlier on. Not only would the apples fill our stomachs but the delectable juices would give relief to our parched throats, driving the dust away and down into our bowls, until further misery can be drawn into our lungs with the continued march. Several men take the opportunity and grab what they can, sergeants turning a blind eye, officers doing the same, but one has to be careful. I later learn that several men are actually charged with stealing, but we look at it as denying the enemy, who would only come to eat and then destroy the trees in any case. My hand moves subconsciously to my breast pocket. There is a card within it. Upon the card is…. Well; an oath: we all have one.

It reads:

Be invariably courteous, considerate and kind. Never do anything likely to injure or destroy property, and always look upon looting as a disgraceful act. You are sure to meet with a welcome and to be trusted; your conduct must justify that welcome and that trust. Your duty cannot be done unless your health is sound. So keep constantly on your guard against any excesses. In this new experience you may find temptations, both in wine and women. You must entirely resist both temptations, and, while treating all women with perfect courtesy, you should avoid any intimacy.

This is signed by Lord Kitchener and so it is an order, not a reminder of any chivalrous code of conduct.

I remove my hand from my pocket in time enough to aid a man beside men: he fell asleep whilst walking.

We are now covering a good twenty to thirty miles per day in the summer heat that beats down upon us as the dust rises. I am reminded again of the weight we carry, although many have already discarded much. It is sheer agony to continue on with all we have been issued but in all cases I draw witness to seeing not a single man throw away his tin of 100 cigarettes.

There are so many cigarettes per man but no one is smoking. There is no time for smoking. Who wants to add dryness to the throat that is caked with dust? But I do see a man gulping down his water as though from a tap when an 'old sweat' pats him upon the back and advises him against it. Ah… you've forgotten… what is an 'old sweat' I hear you ask? A reminder; he is one who has fought before, engaged the enemy in other conflicts. There is many an old sweat amongst us in the battalion, men who have served in South Africa, fighting against the Boar. These men are full of knowledge, full of patriotism, good ideas, unfathomable courage and have a fortitude which stands against the hardest times and conditions. Learn from these men and you learn a lifetime's worth of skill.

It is night, it is time for rest. We gather around and fall quickly to the darkness that is sleep, too tired to even dream.

We are suddenly woken. Have we slept? Yes, we have, but it's time to get going for the enemy is not far behind and we need to be on our way. It's now past midnight and so we are in another day.

28th AUGUST 1914

Today is worse than the day before. Our feet feel the pinch of constant agony, in particular after a ten minutes rest. We would be better without the rest and to continue forever on for our feet would suffer less for it, but we must allow ourselves time to rest if even for a few minutes and to water ourselves like deprived animals. And the days that follow are all much the same. Falling asleep whilst on the march, thirsty beyond belief, sweltering under a midday sun, drawing the dust into our lungs, crying silently at the pain we suffer underfoot.

I can then hear cheering from behind me and I turn as others do. The Scots Greys are coming our way having delivered blow after blow upon the sod that continues behind us. And there are others too for I see lances held in the air. They rush past us and create a light breeze, the thundering of their hooves upon the ground reaching our ears like music. It is sheer bliss to see them, so proud and high in saddle. And then the cheering stops. Towards the rear, and following behind, are not stragglers but men towing horses with empty saddles. We can see without a doubt that they have suffered heavy casualties.

31st AUGUST 1914

Our days of free marching were almost at an end. The time to fight seemed once more to be almost upon us. It would be our turn soon to face the music for the cavalry to date had acted with such exemplary courage and style that the infantry would have no choice but to prove themselves fit for war: though in all truthfulness I may have not said that correctly, for we had no reason to further prove our metal for what we had already achieved at places such as Mons, Le Cateau and Ètreux, but who am I to give praise to oneself.

I shall now tell you this. All three columns at the withdrawal had come to a halt at some time in the late afternoon to early evening; the I Corps was near Villiers and Cotterets, the II Corps near Crepy-en-Valois, and the III Corps around Verberie. These names may not mean much to you, the reader, but to us they meant everything.

The cavalry had done their duty and it would soon be time for us, even though the cavalry was called upon to fill a large gap which existed between the II and III Corps. We would soon continue with the withdrawal on the morrow but maintain good rear-guard actions along the entire defensive line now drawn as we continued towards Paris. Our current position towards the River Marne was approximately a quarter ways past the River Aisne and the rest towards the Marne.

It wouldn't be long now before we started to fall back towards the Marne River along with the French, and the Marne River was placed horizontal to Paris. Imagine Paris; now draw a line out to the east. That is the Marne, and Pairs was literally exposed to a frontal invasion. But our current position was still far from our destination with the cavalry stuck at a place called Néry and employed as gap filler.

To date we'd suffered horrible losses but far more were to come in this war of attrition.

Field Marshall French blamed the losses of the BEF on the French and their inability to hold a line. The French were continually withdrawing, exposing flank after flank, the BEF suffering by such actions, but if it wasn't the BEF that suffered then it was the French. General Lanrezac of the French Fifth Army was equally enraged by what he called our inability to support our ally between Guise and St Quentin through which area the river Oise flowed. It was all finger-pointing to me and all I could hope for was that they would work together instead of apart. In the end it was Kitchener that came to the rescue, insisting that the BEF hold the line as best as possible, which French agreed to so long as the French Fifth Army did not expose another flank as they had done in the past.

We slept soundly this night and were well on the way by morning's first light.

The Action at Néry was upon the BEF and with its disposition upon the ground we were in easy reach of the sound of battle when it opened up, a surprise to all and no doubt those caught in the mayhem that followed.

When battles are fought the news travels fast and in some cases, though fewer than I have been lead to believe, are doted extravagantly with tall tales of heroism and good deeds, but when you see a list of names of those being awarded the Victorian Cross, and that list is extensive for the action fought, then you know all to be true and passed on without the shred of a lie being spoken, and the Action at Néry was one such memorable episode of great historical worth. The units who fought here were again the cavalry units against cavalry, all being dismounted for the duration of the hostile encounter.

Those units present were as follows: the 1st Cavalry Brigade consisting of three regiments: 2nd Dragoons, 5th Dragoons and the 11th Hussars, each with a supposed strength of 549 men with Vickers machine guns in direct support. They were also in the company of the Royal Horse Artillery of 205 men and six 13-pounder guns.

It all started as dawn commenced to break on the first day of September with a fog enveloping the low lying ground between the buffs of the valley in which they were situated, the fog rather stiff in a windless moment of solitude where not a sound did exist that wasn't part and parcel of the great mystery of nature. It was 0430hrs, or there about, and not a soul was stirring other than sentries jostling from their posts and waking all for the day's activities, which included more of the same: withdrawal and rear-guard action.

Men saw to their horses as well as themselves but pride and joy was in the beasts of war that were an extension of the weapons that sat slung over shoulders. Some men prepared breakfast for others whilst others attended the horses. It was a fair trade in particular for an animal lover, but fondness for an animal, in particular a horse, was as dangerous as having many comrades upon which to rely and to be friends with. Death was an awful way to part good company and the loss of a well-loved horse was no less excruciating to its rider. Better to cook the meals for others than get too acquainted with the horses was my point of view.

The men of the Horse Artillery took the time now to ready theirs by harnessing the guns but ensuring they were lowered so as not to press their great weight upon the horses as they supped and watered, for it would be easy enough to prepare for the move towards the south and Paris after this breakfast.

By 0525hrs the 11th Hussars had been ordered with a patrol to conduct a quick clearance of the area towards the south-east, and although this was towards the general vicinity of II Corps a sound of some sort had been heard and interest aroused. To their horror they were confronted by cavalry of the enemy twice the size in number to their own currently stationed at Néry, belonging to the sodding 4th Cavalry Division. I'm sure I have no need to tell you that they scarpered out of their as fast as their mounts could carry them and reported their findings, to which they were ordered to dismount immediately and find themselves positions along the eastern edge of the village to prepare for the hasty defence to come.

By 0540hrs the enemy had opened the hostilities by pressing home thunderous fire which disturbed the serenity, from light artillery and machine guns of the advanced guard, but it wasn't long before the German commander ordered a dismounted attack upon the village of which he no doubt had never heard of until that day.

It was mayhem for the BEF with riderless horses making a run for it and artillery soldiers endeavouring to get their guns positioned upon a firing line of which they managed three from six, two of which were unceremoniously taken out of action as quick-as-you-please. From that moment on it was one British gun against twelve field guns on the ridge to their east from whence the patrol had emerged the fog within the valley, previously. This single gun managed to continue firing until all of its ammunition had been practically exhausted and reinforcement arrived later in the morning, the German artillery seemingly favouring to conduct counter-battery fire as opposed to directing their massive weapons against dismounted cavalry; this in turn provided our men upon the ground much needed fire support by drawing the enemy guns away from opportunity targets.

At 0600hrs the Dragoons made a move to outflank the enemy that our-numbered them and by 0800hrs the British reinforcements [the Middlesex Regiment, the 4th Cavalry Brigade and a battery of Horse Artillery] had arrived to conduct a counterattack upon a demoralised and retreating German division as they were being routed into all directions one could point a stick, leaving their precious commodity behind which entailed eight captured artillery pieces, and due to a lack of horses, all of their food, water and ammunition. The 11th Hussars still full of adrenaline pursued their advantage upon the routed mass and gathered 78 prisoners from which to attain much information of military importance.

Such a grand victory it was in the face of an advancing enemy and superior in number. The surprise of the encounter was obviously the point of imbalance for the sod and so happy we were to know this, but with the action over with the marching continues and ever southward we continue.

4th SEPTEMBER 1914

It looked at first as though Paris would be taken by the sod and the so-far victorious armies as we were, representing the allies as a whole, were literally forced to fall upon the River Marne for defence, but illustrious, good fortune shined down upon us.

Through poor insight the Germans continued upon our heels and on the 3rd continued with the swerve to the left in a move to crush the French once and for all, a total of 150,000 men in the Sixth Army and 70,000 within the BEF. But the manoeuvre was wrought with danger for the German First and Second Army, for their right flank was to become exposed. This was to turn the tables completely in our favour and about bloody time, too.

Again it was Lord Kitchener whose quiet [or not] words into the ear of French assured that he would assist our French allies as best we could and the only way to do this was by performing, as all good infantry must, to the highest expectation in the attack. To perform an attack we must hit the enemy hard [or where it hurts], see a strategic move unbalance the threat, and hit home with continued bouts of hostile fire until victory is so thick that is can be plucked from the air, stuck in a cigar tube and smoked for the pleasure it gives.

We were to go from rags to riches overnight. We were about to exit the most terrible march any of us had ever encountered, where men fell upon their faces, where men tripped over small stones, over each other, banging head into rifle barrels, suffering all manner of deprivation both by day and by night… can I go on, but of course; do I need to, of course not.

Now I know I have promised you more-of-a personal account of action and experience as that which we faced as men of war and combat, and I shall certainly get to it, but some battles need to be painted in order to get to the grind stone of true suffering and conflict. Please bear with me.

5th SEPTEMBER 1914

Although we had put in a good fight by inflicting what appeared to be many more casualties upon them than they did upon us, the withdrawal was unavoidable. After two weeks and 251 miles, however, the tables would be turned momentarily and we would become the pursuer. The well-ordered and executed tactical withdrawal from the advance of the sods was put to a stop. But miraculous achievements don't just happen, and certainly not over a period of minutes or even hours. Good things take time and so did our coming victory to be, which would soon see delivered to us all, four years of trench warfare.

We turned and faced our foe and conducted a counterattack, hand in hand with the French, still with water canteens as empty as our stomachs. We were now at the Battle of the Marne which constituted seven days and nights of warfare. For all intents and purposes it did appear that we, the BEF, had suffered heavily through the incompetence of the French and at the hand of General Lanrezac but Sir John French stabbed back, and rather personally I would consider, by refusing to support the French at Guise. I understand the formalities of an eye for an eye and take no pity on poor souls who are dealt what they justly deserve, but to play games with men's lives by not supporting one another was sheer insanity. At the time I could only hope that it would never occur again, but I too suffer from having a naïve personality at times of greatest need.

Yes indeed; autumn was on its way, the morning was fresh and chilly, and men put smiles upon their faces and lips to rifles as the time to strike back fell upon us. Orders were coming down from higher that an attack was to be mounted on the morrow, but something had happened to change all of that, for someone forgot to tell the sod of our intentions and instead of awaiting our assault the German command decided to overextend their general reliance and over exhausted troops. The entire German First Army was wheeling into a position facing the west, their cavalry hitting the advancing French Sixth Army. The Germans push very hard against the French and in doing so did expose themselves to an attack upon their right flank.

The next few days passed quickly, little time to rest and reload our rifles. The next few days seemed to melt into one another like honey into a teacup – ah… the thought of a single cup of tea.

By the 7th of September, and a besieged French Sixth Army, 10,000 French reserves entered the fighting, 6,000 of which had been delivered to the fight in 600 Parisian taxi cabs as they streamed out of Paris and towards the unstable front line. It was a deciding factor in the downfall of the German advantage, and with the news that there was now a 30 miles gap in the German lines, pursuit was almost on with the BEF taking good measure of what the Allied aircraft overhead advised was a sizeable and attractive opportunity. The sod tried to blow it out of the sky with percussion shells but their fire, at present and for the remainder of the war, was extremely inaccurate. I would hazard a guess that we might have lost a single aircraft to every three hundred shells fired at one but even with these figures it was best to avoid being fired upon.

By the 8th September the French rallied from their past, poor performances and carried out an aggressive attack which further saw the divide between the German First and Second Armies grow at an alarming rate.

The sod was done for. And why was this, why a sudden turnaround in French ability? It was rather simple when you considered that General Lanrezac had been replaced by another. It's not the infantry ability to perform a task which merits victory but the officers to enact and give proper orders, and although the skill of the infantry is a driving wedge which sees an army win in conflict it is only by carrying out orders that such is achieved. But let me say here and now that even a lowly private soldier can have the guts to give orders and see them carried out during hard times.

Even now, as we advanced a few miles here and there, the German atrocities could be seen through our own eyes. Previously we had heard that the German sod did this, and he did that, but to see it with your own eyes was to serve lashings of adrenalin during battle, every man wishing to deal blow after vicious blow upon the retreating bastards. They were running scared now. Where we had carried out a tactical withdrawal they were running with tails between their legs: was I being fair?

Houses with windows smashed, beds and other property thrown out of windows and onto roads, the conscripts had dealt an unfair card. There were victims of crime coming out from hiding, poor women and young girls coming forward to announce that they had been raped, all with tears in their eyes: it hurts the most when the girl is barely into her teens.

Out feet were less sore now for what did we have to complain about? We were only fighting a war but these young girls had to carry the disgusting filth of a memory of forced penetration with them for the remainder of their lives.

I feel sick now and consider the safety of my new family at home. I shall not under any circumstances allow the sod to make it to England for fear of what they might do to those I love the most. Maybe it's this fear that will win us the war.

9th SEPTEMBER 1914

There are not many glorious days in war but when they occur they are so sweet. The sodding retreat of the bastard sons of Kaiser lasted from the 9th to the 13th and not a day during this period went by without a smile to be seen somewhere nearby and the skies with our planes conducting reconnaissance missions to evaluate the situation with the hot pursuit.

Maps in every headquarters… there must have been numerous arrows pointing to the great victory that was the Battle of the Marne, the advancing French Armies and BEF being spurred on by thoughts of the great delivery that fell into our laps, assisted greatly by the 75 artillery batteries of French nationality, a decisive key in the turnaround of historical events as they set themselves before us. No longer would the sod be celebrating a quick and easy victory over the allies by plundering Paris, but now they must prepare themselves for four years of war upon two fronts. Pray to God that the Russians don't make peace too early or out of spite for without their pressure upon the Germans we would be in dire straits.

At one stage it appeared as though the sod was going to be wiped out and that the war would be over but the hate within the conscripts and their higher authority was bent upon bringing misery to all upon a silver platter. Such hatred must be spurred by a venomous breed of man in order for the need for war to be continued. I could not help feeling a great hatred for these men dressed in grey that opposed us but later in the war I would feel as though I understood them for many proved to be more human than me, myself.

The days and nights continued to pave the way for further misery and 12 miles a day was covered, many with the eyes and ears working overtime in an endeavour to see the sod soldiers killed before I bore the brunt of another's anxieties. But we needn't stress too long for the retreat was ceased at a point just north of the Aisne River, some 40 miles of hot pursuit having been completed.

I shall now give you some hasty figures to chew upon; the Battle of the Marne saw two million men trying to kill one another, almost 500,000 were either killed or wounded. I had had a 25 per cent chance of being killed or wounded and yet I lived. I could come through the other end of this misery unscathed: but far more misery was to come.

If I could survive till now I stood a chance of surviving the war. My spirit was lifted. I was becoming a stranger to that thing called fear; but old enemies have ways of beating back upon the back door as unwelcome guests as so the stranger would one day come to haunt me again one day, and that day would not be too far ahead.

Those were feelings that rose from time to time, and happier times were when we saw thousands upon thousands of German prisoners of war being fed through the system and towards our rear, along with much enemy artillery and other supplies. And then I fell upon a poor woman who had a story to tell, one that I still find hard to believe even to this day. She told me of the enemy cavalry and what they had done to her child. They had held him down and used a sword to cut off his legs, but the first attempt missed and cut off his lower limb below the knee and so another attempt was made. Many young girls were also robbed of their virginity. I saw the graves in which they lay, fresh soil heaped upon the face of the earth, forever reminders of war and its horrors.

I could do nothing for her and maybe that was the trick. Was she after sympathy from us soldiers of the BEF or was her story of molestation and rape true? I shall never know. I am torn between truth and lie. I hope the story is untrue so that the idea of so much suffering can be waved aside, but I also hope [and it is not a strong word in this sense] that it is true, for to see someone tell such a lie as that being told, and with such conviction, only achieved a single goal and that was that the hatred within the men that heard the story did rise to greater heights than before, to such a point where they, themselves, might be forced to see greater sin dealt out upon the enemy when the sod surrendered or were captured alive and or brought in wounded.

13th SEPTEMBER 1914

The Germans were digging in and it would appear for all intents and purposes that the war of mobility had stagnated, but this was so more truthful that it could hardly be believed. The war was to become one of attrition, a system of trenches to soon develop between the Swiss border and the North Sea, a continuous [though with small gaps here and there] system of trenches that scarred the earth for more than 450 miles. 450 miles of twisting trenches, elbow bends along the stretch of protection created so that grenades and artillery rounds falling within caused as little damage to life and limb as possible, the extent of each 'straight' line of trench being limited in purposeful design and nature.

The sod had taken to a defensive strategy upon the northern area of the one-hundred foot river, which was said to have been as deep as fifteen feet. There appeared before us a line of fairly steep cliffs which levelled out after sloping ground to meet a plateau covered in thickets and being rather dense in places. The sod had chosen the ground just two miles, give or take, from the crest opposing this river. The Germans had provided themselves a great advantage with marvellous fields of fire in such a position that they were looking in a downward glance upon anything and anyone that made approach.

It was upon the night that a thick fog fell upon us and an advance over the crest brought us into the fields of fire that the sod had arranged so purposely as though born of the ground around them, having crossed the river with much difficulty upon our manoeuvring being placed. The river crossing itself was swathed with dangers. Crossing hastily prepared pontoon bridges with only flickering light to make our way over turbulent waters, whilst praying that you didn't get hit by one of the many pieces of shrapnel or bullets flying here and there, was not the easiest thing to perform. But the night crossing was the least of our great concerns.

As the mist dissipated on the sun rising above the horizon, glares of sunlight streaming in from the east, a network of gun emplacements commenced to shred us to pieces, the sloping ground serving the trajectory of bullets rather unfairly in favour of the sod.

We had been halted and the command to dig in was given.

We were now born to the world of trench warfare, for both armies, those of the allies and axis not considering for a moment any opportunity to back away from upon the ground in which they stood for retreat was a dirty word as I have already expressed in numerous voices.

14th SEPTEMBER 1914

The small and shallow scrapes upon the ground were now to become our home for the next four years. Sir John French gave the order for all men under his sway to dig, dig, dig, and when you can dig no more, then do all you can to make war less miserable by preparing trenches for movement between the front line trenches and those behind. And so we did, we dug, dug, dug. Sergeants ordered groups of men to scrounge all they could in regards to pickaxes and spades, for although our entrenching tools did the job of digging that no man wished to do the tool was rather inadequate and very slow to achieve the goals set before us all.

Shallow scrapes became trenches of seven feet deep. Soon the communication trenches were connected to these. Comforts were seen too, such as sleeping bays within the sides of the trench walls, walls of timber and braces fixed to keep the whole mess from falling in upon it, parapets and even signposts were prepared and erected. And it was good that our defensive position was becoming more stable and better prepared for the Germans had it over us in so many arenas. Their artillery far outshine ours in number, their machine guns and grenades were all along the front line whereby ours were vastly outnumbered; they had trench mortars and rifle grenades that poured out lashings of misery to fall upon us. Even by night the sod was well endowed with flares and other pyrotechnics. Their resupply was rather easy when compared to ours.

But what we had the sod would never achieve: better training, and we were marksman one and all. But this was also a flaw, for although our combined firing might sound like machine gun fire to the Germans, it certainly did not have the same affects, for cones of fire were a great advantage to machine guns which the rifle simply could not attain.

18th SEPTEMBER 1914

You have to forgive me for I forget the date. At some time between now and the 20th some things did occur which are interesting to know, but war is a blur in the mind which recalls only the bloodiest and cruellest of moments. There was much deceit during the war, many heroics performed, many things to be written about, but that is the idea of this text, to enable you to see through my eyes, and so I apologize for not being accurate in all my words but what follows is a strange assortment of actions that occurred at some interval over several days, I think, and I should clarify them but I do not wish to dwell too long on such misfortunes.

There was a fire fight and the trenches were being lashed heavily by German artillery, so much so that the ground vibrated and felt as though I was on a barge within a very rough sea during a hurricane. It was like an earthquake and many times was this experienced; too many to count. The heavy sodding bombardment was in retaliation and in defence against our progress upon taking some ground to our front. It's not important to know the name of the place, for it is too much for me to recall, but it is what occurred that matters most of all.

The attack was over many miles of ground and in places the fall of artillery was rather sparse, and the opportunity was ripe for a German surrender to take place for we were making great progress.

We had, in places along the line, men in trenches, and upon flanks we had men in the fight. Along the miles of trench there were men under fire of small arms, men under fire from artillery, and several bombs even dropped from planes high above, but the greatest of all illusions were the white flags we saw rising high into the air.

A shout rose here and there and was passed along the entire trench, or so it would seem. Can you image what it would be like to be sitting on the steps of the Swiss Alps and receive a message passed on from man to man that the Germans were surrendering but the message was for those several hundred miles away to the north, not for them. It is ludicrous to believe in such a thing but I tell you now that the message may not have reached the Alps but it was passed a long way along the line at battle.

The word was that the sod was surrendering, that a white flag was seen flying upon a bayonet at the end of a rifle [a handkerchief or some other material]; then the message was of more than one, and I could see them filling the air; what a joyous occasion this was.

We were quickly ordered not to fire and so we became ever watchful as hundreds upon hundreds of sod departed their trenches and gave themselves up to the men almost upon them, and in places where there was nothing but no-man's land the sod crossed this to present themselves as prisoners.

It is a strange phenomenon. In the centre of the line the advancing troops of the BEF were moving forward to accept the surrender but towards a flank the Germans were coming to us.

Suddenly the advance upon the trenches had seemed to falter as the flags of white pressed home the reward of a victory fulfilled. More Germans then appeared with hands held high.

At my end of the surrender the Germans had crossed the ground and giving themselves up to us, those men of the BEF who had been passed the order not to fire upon the enemy during this time of transition.

Was this it; was this the end of the war; was it to be over by Christmas?

Those in the line of advance who had been attacking approached the enemy trenches and those men nearer the flanks such as me were to be offered surrender in the trenches which were our own. But something was amiss. What was it? It was the terror of men surrendering. There was not a man who looked fearful. Their eyes did not speak of surrender but of mischief. And then it happened all at once. The men of ours who were at the German trenches were suddenly confronted by hundreds more of the enemy behind the first, these suddenly opened fire upon our men who stood in the open; secondly the sod who had crossed no-man's land to our trenches were suddenly jumping in amongst us and ordering us to surrender to them.

Those British troops exposed in the open were cut down rather heinously and those with me had a fight upon their hands which was close quarter battle fighting at its worst.

I stuck a man with my fixed bayonet, the bayonet becoming horribly stuck. The bayonet had been driven hard into his chest and was lodged within his ribs. I tugged and tugged as shooting continued around me. The Germans were not surrendering but using it as a ploy to take us, not an ounce of acknowledgement of their abuse against their use of the flag of truce being indicated by a single soul from the grey-clad army.

The sod I had skewered was screaming in pain and I had other matters to concern myself with for there was much action being carried out in our trenches. There was hand to hand fighting going on all around me. And so I kept pulling and pulling, and the sod, now upon the ground, kept weeping in screams if agony, 'no, no, no!' I kept pulling but the bayonet would not give way and the action to my rear seemed to be pressing ever closer. I had to do something and quickly, so I fired my weapon and blew his chest apart but at the same time set by bayonet free of the scabbard of flesh and bone encased around it.

Suddenly there was firing from our flank and our boys had regained much initiative by raking the ground before them with machine gun fire from behind their parapets, the Germans falling as though wheat in a field was being harvested.

That is what I remember, that is what I tell you today. War was for heroes and cowards; it was for the deceitful and honest; it was for those that did not know fear and those that sweat at the mere thought of it. War was where normal men turned insane and the insane were woken from their years of sheltered existence.

I still have dreams from time to time of that sod upon my bayonet. I cannot control my dreams.

24th SEPTEMBER 1914

I have advised you earlier of the way in which trench warfare became a part of our life at war, but how was it that the extent of trenches was so vast? Maybe you should consider it a moment; think for yourself how this might occur.

Well, what do you think? I'll tell you. For three weeks or thereabouts following the stalemate at the Aisne River both the Germans and ourselves did try with the greatest effort to outflank one another, to try and encircle the opposition and bring the war to a quick end. And so the sod would try to outflank us and we would retaliate, and then we would try to outflank them and they would counter this with a counter attack, we would move against this and so on and so worth. We also had a name for this: no, it wasn't labelled with a profane name, nor did we consider it as 'shit happens', but it was called 'Race to the Sea'. Each side tried with all their effort to outflank the other.

10th OCTOBER 1914

Almost to a man, apart from a single corps, were we awaiting deployment into our posts. Our staging area prior to this move was between Hazebrouck and Saint Omer – Saint Omer being approximately halfway between Boulogne and Menen, so in effect we were all within 30 miles of the most famous salient in the history of the war where three monstrous battles were waged over many weeks; Ypres. We were currently in France and awaiting a move into Belgium: we were at Flanders.

And so now we have to deal with no-man's land.

And I suppose I should briefly tell you a little about Ypres so that you get a clearer understanding of the situation.

The salient was like half a circle, the convex shape penetrating into what might be considered as enemy territory so that the enemy completely surrounded you and could fire upon the position from any side they wished. The enemy also had the favour of slightly higher ground but more on that much later in the narrative. The amount of ground which the salient stood to take from the Germans was quite considerable for the half-circle of our defensive position penetrated some six miles into enemy territory.

It's a little funny to consider it 'enemy territory' for we were the ones holding the ground, and although there were to be many attempts to dislodge us from the ground on which we stood we were to prove extremely stubborn in our ways.

The salient in effect is the trench system and behind this the town of Ypres sits naked to German artillery fire, for it is near the centre rear that a road enters the system and supplies are made available to those of the defence, which includes replacements for those who have fought for too long at the front. This area of supply transition from storage to stomach and rifle is known as Hellfire Corner [Menin Gate]. It is also well known to all men that this area is to be passed through on the way to the front and on the way from it. You think that fear will mount out of control on your way through this point towards the trenches but I shall tell you how I felt; I felt the worse for coming from the trenches, thinking how horrible it might be to be killed when being provided a little rest and relaxation, or a ticket home for 14 days leave [which you will find out soon enough was something that did not happen very often].

It appeared, for all intents and purposes, that two battalions from every brigade in Flanders were occupying the trenches. There was a system in place which was supposed to run like this: spend four days at the front and then be relieved, to be sent back to the billets behind the lines. There was the opportunity for what was 'leave in England', or furlough, which to be granted once a year was experienced maybe once every 18 to 24 months on average.

I am sure as hell that there were people pulling the strings, allowing hardened soldiers to be maintained at the front whilst sending quartermasters and others back to England up to three times in a single year. There was no justice. In the end we all received the same three medals, whether we served four years at the front or 12 months behind the lines as a quartermaster; but this service wasn't about medals and I think I have already stated such, in a roundabout way.

22nd OCTOBER 1914

Morning routine rarely changed. It was a system which saw each man fed and watered, and weapon cleaned. We would 'stand-to' quite some time before the night was over and wait for the sun to rise. Once wholly in the sky 'stand down' would be given and morning routine conducted. 'Stand-to' lasted for around 30 to 60 minutes. We would also 'stand-to' and 'down' in the evening prior to conducting night routine. Morning Routine: One man might shave whilst another ate, and yet a third would clean his Lee Enfield. To have every man cleaning his weapon at the same time was simply ridiculous for if the enemy chose that moment to attack then there would be no opposing fire to meet them. But there were times when the system was changed in order to meet the strategic needs of the war. Night Routine: Fresh rations would be afforded where absolutely able and even where the front line was on the move – as proved during the final year of the war – the rations would be spared no haste in getting to us with all reasonable measure of consideration and security taken to those work parties in delivering the great sustenance; even if hardtack and corned beef. The field kitchens of the rear seemed to work tirelessly at it, in the billets and the trenches away from the front, and hot food was often taken to the very front: in particular for the benefit of the officers who would be provided all manner of good courtesy at feed time. Quite often the rations to the front came in sandbags with tea, sugar, bacon [cooked or not], bread and the days mail all combined. It was a poor sap who received the parcel from his mum soaked in stew for sometimes the containers in which a stew might be afforded would come undone and ruin everything – but we still consumed it all.

The day wore on as any other, pot shots being taken at the enemy, the Race for the Sea at it ends, the attrition phase of war now commencing to take its toll upon us all. Everything we did was to accommodate this theatre of war, the war of attrition. It was a horrid time but by no means the worst.

At the northern most extremities of the salient at Ypres the Germans were busy laying down an artillery barrage which woke men up quick smart, their clean weapons ready to see action once more and the wait was a short one. The sod was after our trenches, trying with all their effort to drag us from our prized possession and keep it for themselves.

The order were passed around, thunderous voices giving orders to the men on the ground as we watched in eagerness the sod move into position in readiness to attack. "Stand-to! Stand-to! Watch your front for here they come, lads! Mark your targets! Wait! 500 yards; 400; 300. Open fire, ten rounds at the rapid!"

And so the fight was on once more.

Somewhere along the line the sod was successful in his endeavours but our counter attack saw the trenches back in our hot little hands. It was only a small effort by the enemy. Maybe this was a large scale, noisy reconnaissance. It was easy to draw conclusion from this effort of theirs and that was that there was more to come in the morning.

23rd OCTOBER 1914

As any other day preceding it we were hard at work on improving the trenches for the long haul. A single sodding shell making a direct hit could make for hours of back-breaking work. And this day like all others saw many shells falling in our direction. It seems that my hunches in regards to a noisy reconnaissance by force were to be proven correct. But to tell you the truth, so that you can see the picture in your eye as I see it in my mind, there were many trenches which weren't trench like. It was a fact that a lot of the protection from which we fought were nothing more than hastily dug rifle pits and it was the spoil from these that we packed down to act as parapets. Not everyone had the great convenience of a seven foot deep trench with bearings, walls of planks and floors of pellet. Not everywhere on the front was the same as everywhere else.

Our own artillery did all it could to fire back but the area in which the batteries found themselves was as flat as the ground before us and so it was difficult for them to conduct any good and effective means of counter measures. This point was also proved during the years that followed for there were many occasions on which gunners were able to target infantry in the open simply by looking over their open sights; a smorgasbord ready for the culling.

It was on the opening of the evening that the Germans commenced their assault, preparatory fire having been conducted to soften us up, but the Kaiser should learn that the BEF could not be softened by the firing of a few thousand shells for our need to defend our ground was greater than the German need to claim it: therefore I could always see a shadow of doubt within the sods' scheme of things.

42

The sod was coming forward in such dense ranks that it was impossible to miss a target and with the rapid fire capability of weapon and men the enemy were in for a lot of trouble. But they kept on coming as though there was no end to them, coming forward at a walk, climbing over the dead bodies of their comrades as they moved ever forward into oblivion. They seemed not to care: was this because they had some form of political officer behind to force them forward with threats hanging over their heads that any coward was to be shot; I don't know but suspected it: I'd heard of this happening earlier on in the war at Mons.

The poor civilians of Ypres were also hit hard for there were many dwellings; homes of generations passed that were now on fire and crumbling down around their ears… for those so silly to remain inside; but what do you do, hide in the shelter of your home or take to the streets and run along between the shells as they plummet to earth.

The first series of waves had been halted, this was pleasing to see, but it wasn't long before another was on its way and as the darkness of the night came to fall about us all another attack in waves had commenced. But it was due to the hard work of men killing men that we lived. So hard they worked their weapons that it wasn't uncommon to see soldiers throw their weapon aside and to grab another for it was too hot to handle from all the firing. This second attempt at taking our trenches lasted for almost two hours but they were repulsed to a man and we saved the day.

It was hard to believe, this audacity that the enemy had to approach us with weapons firing from the hip, coming at us so slow and recklessly. It was to their undoing, what should I care; honestly.

It is now I quickly duck down and prepare some clips for use in my weapon and as I draw my eyes away from the dead that litter the ground before me I see a young face, a man who arrived just a few days before, being a volunteer as us and a replacement for a fallen comrade: it was easy to be killed; easy to lose a friend and so hard it was to stay alive.

He was a young man and he was crying softly unto his self, clutching his weapon with both arms, the weapon held vertical between his knees. You could see at a glance that his spirit was gone. He was no longer a man but an empty shell. A few days of war had turned him into a shambles. I tried to urge him up, for him to gather his spirit and meet the reality of the day. He needed to fight as we were fighting so that victory would be ours, but he would not move.

It was then that a stretcher bearing party of two came upon the scene and with quick but gentle persuasion took the man away.

I feel guilty now for what that young man had done to me. He gave me courage; he instilled upon me the ambition to forget the fear of death no matter how small because I knew as all men did that you could be brave one day and a mess the next.

So it did seem that the end of battle was upon us this day and the look upon the other men around me was one of great support and merit. Here were men that were suffering as I, and were closer to me than brothers of the same mother. It is wonderful the feeling you get from one another, the idea that you can provide such support in times of need that the fear of being blown to pieces is shrouded by a greater need; to do all you can to aid your comrades in arms. In years to come I would hold in my arms the dying, their blood soaking into my uniform, tears flowing freely from my face. Is it no wonder then that some men prefer, through sheer horror of loss, not to have any friends on the line, for they would be spared the grief that I was to suffer by maintaining good relations with all. Some men were unwilling to make friends with anyone.

It is now time to briefly reflect upon the day, to count our blessings. We had lost many men to the shelling but fewer to the brutality of small arms. And then I see another man standing and watching his front like a good soldier does, but the look upon his face was one of sheer misery. I ask him later what it was that he was thinking and he told me that he didn't want to be killing people, even if they were Germans who had committed atrocities. Killing was not in his blood but rather than see his friends open to the hostility of the enemy he had decided to do his bit by killing as many as he could. He would suffer the memory of these killings in years to come but during times with old comrades he would recall the good times spent at war, and yes, there are a few, believe it or not.

The copses before us were starting to look rather... shrivelled. The landscape was starting to look like the surface of the moon. The flatness and greenery that is Flanders was starting to resemble a desert wasteland of churned up earth. One day the earth of Flanders would resemble little more that life-taking mud; cesspools in which men would fall and die and bloat.

We had held our positions proudly and gallantly, if I may be as bold as to say, and to obey an order given me I provided assistance in getting a wounded man to the rear for some urgent medical attention.

It was a long journey, though not due to distance but the shear effort in supporting another and trying to make gain upon distance through a country marked by killing fields of fire which the sod was happy to sodden with bullets, shrapnel, and our blood.

We eventually came upon the Regimental Aid Post and after a quick drink of water from a canteen, and seeing the line of wounded mounting, I was ordered again to continue on to the dressing station which was reportedly, 'not so far away'. Certainly within the mile it was but took several more hours to reach from my initial point of departure.

Finally, clambering down into the crowded room with straw upon the floor I saw tables on which to carry out surgery and other medical aid such as bandaging. There were many men upon the floor waiting to be seen to and of course the most urgent were seen to first. It was also interesting to note the looks upon the faces of the medical officers, orderlies and surgeons. They all seemed stricken with a slight grief though this was certainly not too overbearing. The reason I mention it is because a year later I happen to be in the same dressing station and although most of the people had changed, which was of no surprise, but the contrast looks upon them all had changed vastly from those early days. It was as though during the early part of the war I saw medical officers working on human beings and that later in the war, the further you went into the misery of this insanity, there was a transition where upon it seemed as though they were working upon dead animals or manikins. At present they were men operating on men, later they would become accustomed to the savagery of war and look like robots operating on sacks of potatoes.

So I reported to a busy orderly and was asked to leave. I stepped further back and looked at the one I had helped. I did not know him but now felt the deepest sympathy, his shoulder wound having caused much concern: more concern than pain. I stood momentarily at the door before turning away., turning my back on an orderly holding a candle in the top of an empty wine bottle as the medical officer took the leg off a man screaming in pain because he'd not had enough morphine, or the fear of losing a limb was too much to bear.

I returned to my place upon the front line.

The following days saw further attacks by the sod, much carried out in a similar manner to before, each wave being cut down with great ease as our weapons overheated in the brutal exchange of ammunition. I knew the conscripts would be short on training but I didn't think they would be short on brains, which lead me even further into my belief that they were being forced to meet their death, that even their officers above them were having their hands tied. And on the 29th day of October I heard a story filter down that the Kaiser himself was bitter about the great loss and our stubbornness to be moved. It was said that he spoke the following words, or similar to them: 'the men of the BEF are trash and extremely feeble, who will surrender in mass if they are attacked with vigour'. I must say that even a speech like that would not have me wanting to conduct wave upon wave of attack upon such murderous fire that we provided. I was also to hear in future years that what the Kaiser had supposedly said was sheer propaganda and made up by British officers in order to get our spirits up. If my spirits were any higher in conviction then I would be an angel.

11ᵗʰ NOVEMBER 1914

Ah; Armistice Day, yet we're not to know it for quite some years to come.

It was coming to winter where misery bore many new names such as freezing fog, prolific lice, trench foot, trench nephritis, and hypothermia. But regardless of these, where there was misery to be had during the winter months it could easily be found. And so on this day we saw the last ditch effort of the sod in trying to take the trenches from us at Ypres before we all, on both sides, settled down to the commencement of the war of attrition, living harsh existences in conditions unfit for anything, it would seem, but lice and rats.

Being with General Horace I was a part of the group assigned to occupy a 17 mile front, Ypres being part of our flank, and so in the following I was not involved.

The Prussian Guard came at us at a faster pace than was normal, seemingly jogging along and actually getting to our trenches in places where hand to hand fighting would be pursued, but their attempt was the same as previous weeks and they were sent back to their own lines with far less than they had started.

The fortifying of trenches and elaborate bunker systems was now carried out, none so fine as the Germans for their bunkers, particularly at the Somme, would prove to be outstanding achievements under such hostile fire that we could manage to send them. But you shall learn of these a little later on.

Further hard work was to be mustered in the direction of field defences, namely barbed wire. Erected at night these were a hazardous task to complete, too much sound and the sod would put up a flare and find you out with machinegun fire. But between the last effort of the sod to take the trenches and the continuing effort to construct field defences and other obstacles came the opportunity to rest a little, in particular during the day.

24th DECEMBER 1914

The days leading up to Christmas of 1914 were intense to say the least. The war was supposed to have been over by now but here we were, in the cold of the night and day living like morbid creatures trying to keep warm. The scenery was always the same, the trench, for it was almost impossible to look over the parapet and not be shot at by an enemy sniper, or some German with a rifle trying to show off how efficient he was at shooting over iron sights. And then I did a fool thing, I looked over the top of the trench to see what I would make of no-man's land during the day, for very little could be made out during the night.

I could see one of our men who had received a bullet to the head not so long ago whilst out on a mission – or fools task – to repair a gap in some wire due to an enemy trench mortar. He had a dozen rats or more eating his flesh, they had started from his toes and head, and were working their way both up and down to meet in the middle, as though in systematic operation with one another, refusing to touch certain parts too foul to mention, but I must in order to give you the full picture; they refused to touch any part of the human body that contained faeces. My only wish was to pick up my rifle and shoot the damn things but I couldn't; not only would the firing bring machine gun retaliation but we had orders not to harm the damn things because they helped to keep the battlefield nice and clean. No one enjoyed the smell of death; it was a most disturbing thing to have to experience. But no matter where you looked the rats were at work, literally thousands upon thousands of them nibbling on every carcass there was between the two lines of trenches; and they are absolutely huge in size.

Now, I have heard a story that the rats will never touch a living man, even if asleep, but I tell you now that in the dead of night of my first winter in Flanders I was rudely awoken on at least one occasion by a rodent trying his luck. They had come after the rations [I have no choice in considering this the reason] which, when we have them to spare, are suspended in sandbags from the supporting beams of dugouts where officers are concerned, and so I assume that on their way past me they chose to try for a quick nibble. Imagine his fright to get a punch to the body. Image my fright and be woken in such a way. I can still see that rat in my illuminated imagination saying, 'sorry kind sir, but I meant not an ounce of discourtesy towards you for I thought you were dead'. And sometimes I thought I must have been.

And speaking of courtesy, there were no attacks during the winter months. But on reflection I'm sure this has nothing to do with courtesy at all.

25th DECEMBER 1914

How could one be so courteous to an enemy? It sounded... foolish... no, no... it sounded simply barbaric to be courteous to someone who had caused so much death and misery, but on reflection I assume the sod must be thinking the same. But then for Christmas Day this year we were all treated to the hospitality, of which I and several others refused to accept, of the enemy in no-man's land: they called it the Christmas truce of 1914.

How could this form of fraternization come about?

The Germans were reportedly the second largest population of all immigrants in England prior to the war and it was often heard that students and young men of English origin went abroad to Germany for a good dollop of education: though I see nothing wrong with the education I received.

And so they met in the middle of no-man's land, between the opposing lines of trenches scarring the earth, to exchange food, cigarettes, good song and commiserations. It is all for nought at the end for on the morrow we shall all be back at the throat of the other, shooting each other with rifle, blowing each other up with bombs and artillery, and generally having a good go at killing the man in the opposing trench.

3rd MARCH 1915

Winter was over with at last and the sun gave increasing amounts of heat for us to be warmed as each day passed into the next. I seldom forgot what day it was. It didn't seem to matter that much but when an important day was coming up fast then I would always put extra effort into trying to remember the date.

Our trench system had been improved markedly over the winter months, working by night and sleeping by day; we were also moved around on occasion, back to the billets for a few days, back to the front line again for a few more, and when you returned it was either to a slightly better prepared trench then when you left it or to one that had hardly been touched and needed much work carried out upon it. I didn't mind the idea of working hard to fortify our position and trying to make it more comfortable, but I didn't like working fingers to the bone when others seemed to be sleeping the war away both day and night as opposed to helping his fellow man by digging.

Although the trench system was still not unbroken from one end to the next and gaps did exist here and there [which saw some men, from both sides, getting lost and passing through to the other side of no-man's land] they did resemble the great artefact which was the war of attrition.

Other than the departure of winter there was another reason for us all to wear a smile upon our faces for our good friends from Canada were preparing to move into the line and by the 3rd day of this month being introduced to the trenches. Ah, how marvellous it is to see such a grand example of courage and friendship.

We had the honour of passing over our portion of the trench and managing several newcomers to the new way of life which was to be endured by them. One of them kept going on about having a look over the top so that he could look upon no-man's land but we insisted that he keep his head down because there were many snipers in the area. I recall looking once myself but since that day have stuck with the periscope. I handed it to him.

He didn't seem too pleased with having to look upon the enemy through a periscope and so lifted his head then to see the entire area void of any movement even though in all reality the opposing trench works would have been swarming with the sod.

The newcomer seemed to draw a little confusing on seeing so little action and lifted himself a little more and then we heard the shot and got showered in his blood and brains. I recall having to scrape flesh from my khakis in great distaste. From that moment on they kept their heads down but the length of the line they had moved into was vast and so there were several shots heard ringing out as German snipers targeted their victims.

16th MARCH 1915

Although winter was over with I could not say the same for the rain. The rain itself could be lived with but what it brought with it was much misery.

The mud was one aspect; you simply could not get it off you. The boots we wore weighted in excess of ten pounds, or so it seemed. Walking along in some of the trenches was one way to see a little light at the end of the tunnel for the rain would fill the trenches so that you couldn't see the floor boards you were walking upon, and in some cases you couldn't even see your knees because it was so deep; and yes, it got even worse than that.

Trench foot was ever present, its ugly head appearing at every turn. We were normally forbidden to take our boots off during times of great evil for it was often too hard to get the boots back on again after the foot had swollen. But where the strategic element didn't pose too much difficulty, or the time for a possible enemy attack – or our own upon them – had expired, boots came off. It was very painful.

Lessons were learnt quickly in the trenches and passed along for the comfort of all concerned. During times when supplies were brought up from the rear, usually with meals, clean socks were exchanged for the ones we had been wearing or currently had on our feet. A quick and painful change of socks wasn't something we enjoyed doing so we also put plenty of effort into assuring that we were ready. When push comes to shove and hast was written on the walls then two men would pair up. They would put themselves opposite one another and take boots off. Quickly remove the others socks, dry their feet for them, rub whale oil in where available, on with clean socks and back on with the boots before they swelled. The pain suffered in the exchange was a little better put up with when the feet weren't as swollen.

Even so, when socks were changed we would coat them in whale oil, where available, for this seemed to help us in our combined misery. Our dirty socks would be taken back with any rubbish, letters, and sick [though seldom I saw amongst us lot a man volunteering to go sick], the socks to be cleaned and then recycled back to us.

It's a funny thing. A man didn't like to shirk his responsibility by going sick on his mates, for we were volunteers as I have already provided your ear, but when it came to leave then we could not wait to be leaving the trench behind. Of course, leave was very seldom received but it was well earned, a hundred times over, and so anyone going on leave received a good smile and hearty handshake. A comrade never knew if he might see you again and so we always departed on a high note of congratulations and good cheer.

The Canadians, or so I heard, were enjoying their new friends the lice and rats. It had only taken a few days for the entire force of Canadians to be well endowed with condominiums in which the lice lived in luxury and warmth with as much food to chew on as they could ever dream. Many men tried burning the eggs of the lice from the seams of their uniform with candles, seemingly burnt from both ends for it achieved no victory over the uninvited guests. Some men preferred the sod over the lice, but if it wasn't for the sod then none of us would have been here in any case. This and many other incidents within the war, I felt, required recording and so I try to do just that.

I couldn't resist the historical opportunity and took some photographs with the 'Vest Pocket Kodak' which was first manufactured by Kodak in 1912. I couldn't afford one alone by I had other family members who thought it might be interesting and so sent me one – of which I had to take great charge and treated with excessive niceness. It was the size of... about twice the size of a packet of cigarettes and encased in a metal skin with lens. I was quite distraught when hearing the following news:

It would seem that the higher authority didn't like the soldiers, NCO's and officers sending photos back to their loved for it showed the horrors of the war which soiled the news from of the cabinet at large, however, they advised us that the reason for the blanket of security was to deny the enemy any information that they could attain from such photos if the soldier with them was captured. An order had just been received this day that ensured the use of the VPK would be put to an immediate halt. No cameras were now permitted to be used by any person or any unit travelling into war zones overseas.

So much for fair play. I saw very few photos being taken from that day forward but I also saw an increase in the 'blind eye' being employed by officers for their were a few who believed the that the men deserved, and should, secure the history of the war through pictures.

17th MARCH 1915

I must say for the record that the Canadians proved over the coming months to be an extremely brave bunch of men and they did all they could within their power to ensure that the Germans got back what they dished out, and in oversized proportion, but it was these early days of the introduction of war that saw some tight moments play out between them and us: members of the BEF.

All along the front, but not in all places as we were to learn, there existed an unwritten law of policy between the two forces facing one other that dictated as follows, 'live and let live'. The live and let live policy it was, something we had put into place over the winter months and still lived by. I don't know who first thought of the idea but it was sheer brilliance. If only the politicians and other high ranks could see this as a means to bring peace to the table.

The policy meant that we could sleep, and lift our heads out of the muck for a few moments of solace without the fear of being rudely woken or shot at, but the Canadians were somewhat shocked when they first heard of the live and let live policy.

I recall hearing of one man and his experience. A Canadian was cowering [certainly not normal for them] in his trench, shaking from the violence of the shelling going on all around him, when suddenly it stopped as quick as it had started. He took an opportunity to look over the parapet whereby the light illumination from the moon allowed him to see some enemy at work on their wire. He wanted to pick his weapon up and start blazing away, to shoot all he could, to spill some blood, for his weapon was as virgin as he. He couldn't figure out why he'd been prevented from shooting, a calming hand placing itself upon his shoulder and requesting that he stop what he was about to do; but why? The live and let live policy was then explained to him, explained in full how we had enjoyed a little peace after almost a year at war. He complied but was not happy.

Not long after the Canadians were moved [and I think it was in early April] into their own position did they turn the cold shoulder upon the policy and commenced to do as they willed against the enemy to their front.

The sod came to hate the Canadians more than any other. They hated the Canadians for being so brave and forward; they hated the BEF for their proficiency with bayonet and rapid firing; they hated the French for being French, but most of all they hated their Generals: or so I was to learn in the years after the war.

The next four weeks was much the same and nothing of any great importance is worth noting during this period. But it was coming up to April and the Second Battle of Ypres was almost upon us. With many things, however, their must be some form of prologue.

13th April 1914

The BEF and those heroic Canadians who manned the trenches around Ypres were mostly suppressed by view from the Germans, who, having hold of the higher ground did use their tactical advantage always to our misfortune.

I'm sure as hell that it baffles the mind of the sod as to why we held onto the salient of Ypres, for there was little to be gained, strategically speaking. There was little hope of defending against an enemy breakthrough of any superior model and withdrawal to the opposite side of the canal would be undertaken in a whisper. It is here that I learnt that Sir Horse, my cherished commander of great insight, did wish to move the entire front line: but even in this I cannot be overly sure but I know that withdrawal was on his mind, a withdrawal which others of higher command would learn about in the days to come. So why did we hold the unthinkable line of trenches? Because it was the last semblance of Belgium, the last town of this Flanders land that was not currently under sodding rule. This town of Ypres was a reminder of our great courage and determination. We must hold the line here and now, even if it is too ridiculous for a sane man to consider it overall use and value: but some things hold value of the mind, and that is precisely what Ypres was to us.

When the Canadians, only a third of which were born of that land for most came from Great Britain on the trail of immigration, they inherited trenches which were nothing but potholes on a baby's behind when compared to those in other places. There was enemy aircraft to contend with as they dropped bombs and the enemy trenches were only 150 to 300 yards away. And this is what confuses me. It was said that the French believed in an offensive war, but believed in withdrawing to allow their artillery to hold back the surging Germans when they attacked, and so saw no reason to build extravagant fortifications: but in some places they operated quite differently, and I believe that the slopes of Switzerland told a different tale, completely. We of the BEF on the other hand were taught to act in the defensive, for this is where we had proven to be most effective against the Germans, a strong reliance on counterattack being more of a tradition that anything else. Either way you look at it the ground we held in 1914 was pretty much the same as in 1917. Maybe if we'd had more and better artillery during the early stages of the war we could have done something different with the manner in which we conducted the business of this horrid war.

There was also another moment of history to recall of this date and that was the German soldier, August Jäeger. The man deserted his country for some reason or other and at the young age of 24: it appeared at first to have been a ruse of some description for he was extremely adamant that the sod was going to gas the entire line along Ypres and then attack the ground with gusto. He even went as far as describing how it was to be done, the main signal for the release of the gas being three red flares that would be sent skyward as command to proceed. All they needed was favourable weather conditions. August then showed the allies a respirator made of gauze and cotton, advising that all the assaulting troops had these in their possession to ward of the asphyxiating effect, but first they must be soaked in a chemical in order to work effectively. And do you think the allies; those officers at headquarters listening to the tale would listen? Of course not; it was too absurd to be true, even if August did have a respirator with him.

17th APRIL 1915

With the idea of such a gas attack being pushed aside, and no forewarning being given to the soldiers within the trenches, the mammoth task of mining beneath hill 60 continued [little more than sloping ground, really; not a hill at all]. It was from here that spotters drained away the souls of the men of the BEF, static positions for snipers, and generals to draw up plans.

It was in the evening on this day that five tonnes of explosive were detonated and three large craters added to the landscape. It was so loud that even from where I stood, which was nowhere near the hill, I was stunned by the seemingly immeasurable sound. Wave after wave of man after man rushed the hill and took it. The Germans, knowing the great importance of the hill, and like us British, didn't like to give ground away so easily, conducted a counterattack, from which we conducted a counter, counter attack, and the Germans a counter, counter, counter attack, and for what seemed like eternity to the men fighting the battle it seemed like days, and of course there was a lot of killing, but in the end the hill was lost and the sodding bastards stood once more upon the ground of their choosing. But in the midst of this precious fighting was something more sinister which was to occur.

20th APRIL 1915

The fighting upon the sloping ground known as hill 60 was continued without breath for fresh air when a massive bombardment ensued, all the ground encompassing the Ypres salient seeming to be smeared in hell with debris and dirt flying high into the sky. The carnage was horrific. I had heard that in medieval times they launched cattle at one another from trebuchets and the like, but to see men flying through the air, torn limb from limb, is something that is much worse and could never be celebrated: but some of us might be of different mind when seeing the teenagers of today trying with all their mite to prove how absurdly insolent they can be, laughing at heinous scenes of men being killed on the TV screen or at the cinema. I don't think I need to tell you that it isn't romantic.

The bombardment was considered a measurable response to the three craters made by us. But the sod was stepping precariously too close to the edge, for there was no room in war for the killing of civilians, but that is what they did. They destroyed a most beautiful town and many of its citizens. Until that day there were many that suffered profusely in order to stay in their homes but the German shelling had turned nasty and made up the mind of many men and women in regards to overstaying their welcome in their own homes. But for those that decided to stay, they did not stay long.

22 April 1915

The Second Battle of Ypres consisted of four major battles spread over 33 days. The Battle of Gravenstafel was from 22nd April to 23rd and I was not there to see what manner of poor judgements – and some would say heinous – that the damn sods were conjuring up and performing for the sake of their generals' sick minds.

I was not yet on the front line at Ypres but I would be soon enough. It was 1700hrs and the French were being assaulted…. The French are from Martinique, an island of the Caribbean Sea of just 436 square miles; even these men of unfathomable courage see to their duty as all good men do and on the grapevine I hear that something is amiss. The ranks are breaking, running from the greenish-yellow mist which fills the air over such a vast area that the retreat forces a seven kilometre gap in the allied defences.

Why are they running from a smoke screen? Is there something others on the adjoining flanks cannot see? Are there waves upon waves of Germans on the attack? No. Nothing can be seen except the smoke that fills the air. And so the trenches are abandoned quick smart, left to the Germans if they should take good advantage of the situation, but even they are not moving. There is no German assault. The Kaiser, those dirty sods, is not making good the vacated positions. It then dawned upon me as I heard this story and before being told, just for a moment in time, that the smoke screen is something more than I have first considered and assumed. Why would brave men retreat from trenches, whether good or bad?

But some hearts of steel soon restore faith within the minds of all for it is brought to their attention, colourful NCOs and officers of good character offering words of encouragement, and the 1st Canadian Division, along with remnants of the French, have retaken the trenches left so hastily behind and the land is reclaimed once more, though considerably more sparse in man power than existed before.

The soldiers to a man saw the smoke fill the air, thick and fast, 168 tons delivered in 5,730 cylinders [which I would come to learn in the future, for when something so heinous occurs on your doorstep you are prone to find out about it as surely as you are born, live, and then die]. My stomach turns at hearing the cracked voice of the 'old sweat'. Somehow I wish I was at sea and that the bell would toll 'it's five O'clock and all is well', but all is not well and I am tired, as all are, of this stinking predicament in which we find ourselves. And then I comically consider whether or not they would say 'five O'clock' [1700hrs] for I am not at sea but a landlubber through and through. Such ridiculous thoughts inhibit the mind, more so to be rid of this insanity called war. But it seems our duty now to live and die for king and country, but the king would not wish death to fall upon us: not such a thought is considered when reflecting upon some of the generals within our courageous army but even they, too, must consider the larger picture, even at the expense of human life.

And so we see that chlorine gas has been used for the first time but we know it won't be the last. The first step towards great villainy has been taken and cannot be retrieved.

Oh, my dear God! It was dusk when the gas attack occurred. The men in the trenches and those on the run can smell something similar to pineapple and pepper before coming under effect of the gas, and it is so thick in many places that it is hard to see the sod as he exits his trenches and comes towards the ally's line. Who can blame them for running: not I? And although there was no initial German assault the ranks of the enemy now spill out of their trenches. The Germans follow the gas cloud some 15 minutes later and have their masks on but don't breathe easily; there are also many who have the masks simply resting upon their heads in order to fight easily. The masks restrict, are a pain to wear, but worse still is the fear that the effects of the gas might just well fall upon them as well; so why do they advance so?

No matter where one would care to look the scene is the same. Men are falling all over, severe pains in the chest, burning in their throats. They can hardly breathe, poor bastards. They drop like flies, 6,000 dead in ten minutes. The pain; the liver damage; years of misery to come for those that survive, although there are few that can consider themselves lucky, even though they wished themselves dead to alleviate the suffering imposed upon them.

I have heard and seen many atrocities, but what do you call it when a German yanks the weapon you carry in your arms as you crouch their dying from gas and says to you to lie still and die better? It is understandable in some cases to see why it is not practicable to take prisoners. All the prisoners the Germans might want are before them but they are all dying. Why take a dead man prisoner?

The French on the left flank of the Canadians have also abandoned their positions, along with more than 50 artillery pieces, guns which must be taken back over the coming days if at all possible. If the sod is smart he'll destroy them all, or set booby-traps.

I can imagine the men at the billets now, playing soccer or a game of cards, resting on their behinds and eating a hot meal. I can see them now hearing the news of poison gas and each and every one of them looking at each other and asking what the hell is poison gas. It must be as much of an uproar at the billets as on the front, but at the billets they will be preparing for battle whereby those at the trenches are trying to escape from it.

The gas attack upon our brothers was nothing shy of an incurable shock as wave after wave of insurmountable struts of fear struck each and every one of them in mass and by turn. First a few would come under effect and then the masses would learn. It wasn't a lesson to be taught over a pint at the local for the learning curve was so acute that is was practically, and for all intents and purposes, non-existent.

How such a thing as this could be allowed to happen. Weren't generals, and other leaders who never dared to take step upon the battlefield, supposed to consider all factors of engagement prior to practical use; but there was no practical way of expressing how such a demon like poison gas could have been allowed to escape the chamber of its existence. Lying dormant and ready to maim and kill this gas was delivered within projectiles; within shells of the German artillery. Were these sane men that stood opposite us; but no, that couldn't be? I recalled how they had exposed themselves to undue good cause by allowing us to kill them in their thousands during the retreat from Mons. And although I was not present during the early days of Mons I was still to learn from experience for there was no other moment in time that I could recall where men around me would express how similar it was that these bastards took orders from their officers to assault us in waves, to be gunned down like flies with a poison of their own to contend. How could it possibly be that mature men who commanded over a million troops could authorize the use of such a weapon that was lashing out at us in such silence as now?

We would come to learn of many factors in regards to gas exposure during the four years of war in and around France and Flanders. So many names to so many variants existed but all in all it made little difference, for the fear was always the same and could hardly be quelled, and such quelling came in forms of protection which were quick to be granted us, protection which would allow us to kill these bastard Germans who were soldiers just like us: maybe not just like us. Maybe we were a special breed, for we were fighting for different ideas and when your back was against the wall the true colours of the Union Jack came to full fruition. Our blood was not red but red, white, and blue. We fought for the country we loved, for family which was so dear to us all. To me and many others it didn't matter a sod after the Battle of Albert [the Somme] that there was a piece of paper with signatures upon it declaring that England would abide by its treaty and attack German forces as duty declared in the defence of others. I was here for many reasons, including the men beside me, but most of all I was here to see justice done, to see the innocent protected, to see a bright future cast from our combined miseries in order for unborn children and grandchildren to bear the fruits of our sacrifice. These men beside me, although time spent at training is far different than that spent at war, and which I was to learn solidly over the coming years, that comradeship and general friendship, even towards those that you had little in common with on civilian street, were like twin brothers, men that you cared about more than you cared for yourself. But I also knew from stories told that such feelings of devotion would subside and the experiences of the trenches to come could never be felt again with the power that was currently on the climb at a rapid rate. It is a for a variety of reasons that we find ourselves here, that is true, but for the vast majority, and to answer the question, it is for the man beside you; for those of your platoon, company and division that you suffer as you do and fight to the death with tooth and nail. Although we would love to feel that it is for king and country we all know deep down and after long years of fighting that we do not fight for king, or for devotion to the country we love.

You might well tell me that only a small percentage of those men, like me, exposed to such heathen weapons of war died from such exposure, but what of the wounded.

Towards the end of this war the use of gas was so widespread that it was hard to fathom such; even we, the men of the civilised world, did banter and partake in the dreadful use of poison gas. Our philosophy was an eye for an eye. If they bomb us to hell then we shall bomb them back; if they should gas us then beware, you shall not reap the sweet reward of victory for the stone will be cast right back.

Wasn't it a strange thought, that good always seemed to prosper over evil in the same way that hard work always rewarded those hardest at it and the lazy of the earth dwelled in squalor: but there are always the lucky few but we are referring to statistics and percentages, and the percentage at the moment is that poison gas delivered a three per cent death rate to our ranks, a double-edged weapon which would sometimes, with the unpredictable changing of the wind, wrought havoc upon those so ready to employ the gas in the first place. Statistics didn't stop there however for two per cent of the total gas fatalities were made permanently invalid with seventy per cent more than usually able to return to the field within six weeks of contamination; but then again maybe I am wrong. It was a silent killer and seemed to work hand in hand with nature, nature which didn't seem to appear before our eyes on many occasions for the landscape around us was bare of any natural ensemble of woods, grass, flowers or wild animals. How wonderful it would be to see a bird fly by right now.

I had heard, and even now deliberate considerably upon the past, that the French may well have initiated the use of gas by delivering to within the German ranks a tear gas in such small quantities that it was barely noticeable, sent over-the-wall, so to speak, in 26mm grenades. It is to consider whether this was a torment which preluded German behaviour or something else rather benign. Surely a tear-inducing agent was fair in war and would allow the enemy to be bayonetted more efficiently, and fell short of going against the Hague Treaty of 29th July 1899 where three main points of interest gained my attention in later years: That the contracting powers agreed to abstain from using projectiles for the delivery of asphyxiating or deleterious gases; that the declaration be binding in the case of war between two or more of the contracting powers, and; the agreement would cease to be a binding agreement where, in the case of war a belligerent should be joined by a non-contracting power.

I see now that the French in August 1914 could well have induced the fear we all now suffer on a day to day basis, outing into the minds of our adversaries this heinous weapon of mental and physical destruction. I could only wish that the Germans had continued with their initial and nonthreatening attacks of October 1914, for their use of gas was as detrimental as the attacks of August and meant very little to anyone. It would be fair to say that only in the darkest crevices of the most insane mind could the thought of a gas possible of killing thousands should be produced and delivered upon the battlefield, yet the Hague Treaty could see well the future to come. What ever happened on the Russian Front I do not know, but hearsay has it that 18,000 shells containing gas was fired at the Russians in January: but I heard nothing more of this – such wicked things were shunned by me for by the end of the war I had truly had enough. My mind had determinate to the point of near insanity, on the edge of the abyss, at the point of no return, but I somehow saved myself for the days to come where married bliss would see me with a large and loving family. But back to the war I must tread for the story is only just begun.

Everyone across the great expanse of the front had soon learnt the truth of the situation however, as news of the situation reached the ears of every man, woman and child, and that were that the smoke was a poisonous gas.

I am lucky and feel that way, but that irritation of guilt fills me like a sieve choking up with filaments that form a thick screen, and I know that it will be my turn soon enough, for the Germans are a sodden lot. They claim that the attacks do not go against the treaty of 1899, that there is no violation of international law, for what they are employing are not chemical shells but gas projectiles. It is a ridiculous way of looking at the situation but all tied up in the German soldier's character for the conscript he is, so wrought with wrong doing that theft, rape and murder are scenarios that replay themselves time and again in countries like Belgium. Yes indeed, the Germans are a sodden lot for what they have done and continue to do. How can they ever be forgiven?

Men drew deeper breaths as they ran and in doing so found death knocking upon their doors all the sooner. Try as they might they could not outrun the gas which was spreading as fast as the wind could carry it, about 6 miles an hour. Imagine if you will, running along with the cloud of poisonous gas at your back and as it catches you, you try all the more to out-distance it. Death would have been all the easier if the men had stayed in the bottom of their trenches: maybe even survived. Eyes are wide open, the look of shock and terror upon their faces as they cough and cough so heavily, substance like glue pouring out their mouths in many cases. The men were being asphyxiated. Here they are, running for dear life, the town of Ypres in the background burning with fury as flames lick the town clean from the landscape in many places.

People were running and screaming, carrying the young and old, buildings collapsing around them and the gas cloud not very far away. But they were too concerned for their welfare and dodging of bombs to be concerned with a damn smoke screen for behind that would surely be the sod coming upon them at the run. But this wasn't the case, although the gas cloud could be considered a smoke screen, the sod were 15 minutes behind it.

And so the men continued to retreat in overwhelming panic and the horses of the artillery were absconded and employed to get the hell out of there, the guns left behind, for men were more important than artillery. Others dropped all their gear but the few that were so overwhelmed they had gone almost insane with terror and pain, had forgotten to get rid of their burden upon their backs.

By 1900hrs the sod had taken much ground and had crossed the Steenbeck, approaching St Julien. It was here that the Germans suffered a vast majority of their casualties for the 10th Filed Battery of 18-pounder guns could see the massive column of Germans moving across the ground some 300 yards away, a moving target in the open, a site for sore eyes, an opportunity of a lifetime. And so with iron sights and quick hands the artillery took to pouring ammunition into the fray. The enemy were obliterated but many more existed in and around the vast area known as the salient.

It was now becoming quite clear that there existed within the frontline a gap of some 8000 yards, or thereabouts, split into sectors: roughly speaking there was a 2000 yard gap, a 1000, and a 3000 [yes, that's right, adds up to 6000, but its extent is what was of greatest concern, for flanking was a favourite way in which to attack an enemy]. It seemed that the enemy were winning but then they stalled: at around 2000hrs they stalled.

Why did they stall; why did the attack appear to falter? It couldn't have been casualties alone because the Germans cared very little, or so it seemed, about the loss of a few thousand conscripts. Regardless of this I wish that the others in which Smith-Dorrien, the Horse, was sharing his table at dinner would

65

have seen the light in contrast to rumours of gas and have withdrawn to a position just beyond the canal.

I later learn that the sodding attack has slowed to a crawl, and to a stop in places, because the Germans have advanced into pockets of their own gas and wearing the masks upon their heads, as most of them do, they are becoming weary: it is true to say that the crude respirators were not so efficient as the higher ranks would have liked. Two miles of ground they have taken and suddenly there is a moment's pause. More and more of them were coming under the effects of the gas and the scene around them didn't provide much comfort, for they could see the dying faces of the French and Canadians as they either died on the ground or thrashing about for air.

The sod had become a victim of his own creation.

But there is something else that I learn to appreciate and that was the unwavering success of the gas which was completely unexpected. The Germans had advanced as far as they had been ordered to advance and used the gas as a means for which to halt and dig in. the shoe may have been on the other foot had their respirators worked as well as they should have, and the advance may have been undertaken to exploit their current position and route the allies even further afield.

And again, one more note to remember and this being the most important; the sheer courage of the Canadians cannot be expressed enough for even those slightly affected by the passing gas, holding out in the bottom of their holes in the ground, or having the sheer good fortune not to have been hit by the gas at all, stood their ground to repel the sod at every point that he could. So here you have many pockets of resistance standing to fight against the power of the axis as they falter here and there. The Germans knew full well of the BEF and their ability with the Lee Enfield and bayonet as much as they knew the hard core within the Canadians for many lived in the wilderness, were lumberjacks, and carried more muscle upon their huge frames than they carried in equipment upon their backs.

The sheer terror felt by the Germans, for all manner of reason, was the reason for the garrison of 50,000+ men of the salient to have survived. The sod had come so close to capturing the entire salient and 150 guns: so close but no cigar.

It was now dark and although the air was filled with the sounds of war the assault had stopped at every point. The wounded were now evacuated. It is here that many disturbing scenes are met. Can you imagine coming upon a man who is sitting there with his back to the wall of the trench with weapon in his hands as though ready to get up and discharge another clip of ammunition, and then on second glance you look upon him further for he hasn't answered you request for aid in helping a wounded mate. You then shake him and realise that he's dead; his head pierced with hot shrapnel and having dies instantaneously? It is amazing how men die. It is as though some of them have been frozen in life, a wax model of their true selves performing some duty or another; but dead. It is something that dreams are made of that haunt you forever.

23rd APRIL 1915

It wasn't long before we heard filtered words of wisdom from higher, trickling down to us; the men in the trenches. For the moment we were to take preventative measures from the effects of the gas, to avoid the poison substance afloat the wind at all costs. I didn't need an officer to tell me that, but I did need them to tell me what to do; after all, it's no use taking a bucket to a horse at feeding time if the bucket is empty.

Instructions soon filtered down that a wet handkerchief or some other form of cloth, held over the mouth as you breathed, would be sufficient enough to protect us from mild saturations of poison gas. If it was a high concentration then we were reminded of our service to king and country and that we were of the British military. This was well and good and believed by all I knew, but it was a hard pill to swallow when the gas came towards you at 6 miles an hour, able to outrun most men clad in the equipment of war.

Buckets of water were soon delivered the trenches to be used against the gas, or we could urinate upon a handkerchief and hold this against our mouths; either would be appropriate until better means could be secured. Even the nuns at the convent at Poperinge started to give good aid by making lint bandages for us to use, and by the time fresh rations were being delivered on the evening of 24th we were most thankful to the brides of Christ, but that was still a day away yet, at present it was only 0100hrs. 0100hrs and the fighting continued with the allies trying to take back ground and fighting for survival.

I cannot tell you too much of what happened this day for I am a part of the counterattack. We are moving into position and on the morrow will enter battle once more. I feel as though I am an old soldier now and we have many new faces. I help the new ones as best I can because it is hard to know what to do in trench warfare, for little is taught about it back at Aldershot, but sometimes I feel as though getting too acquainted will bring misery later on. Regardless of these feelings I carry on as best I can for we are all here to help one another and without such help I might very well not survive the war.

24th APRIL 1915

The Battle of Saint Julien started today and ended on the 4th or May. It is no more difficult to recount than any other part of the beginning of the war because even though I am getting used to it, but by the time it is over I am like a robot and have accepted that I shall die sooner or later and so find it harder to recall incidents. Imagine my sheer joy at finding myself still alive at the war's conclusion.

The Royal Dublin Fusiliers, of which you'll be kind enough to recall I belong, are almost at the point of being employed in the thick of battle, but we find that we have a single day's reprieve as we prepare. But the war goes on and so the tale must continue.

What can I tell you of the chlorine gas, very little in fact, in particular at the time of the attacks, but there was a chemist within the Canadian ranks [from Flanders Fields] who did well to work it all out, though one might say he knew from experience of its characteristics. I was also wounded by the gas but not today, so fortunate I was. But having been a sufferer of an attack in the near future to come I have licence, I believe, to understand something of the suffering.

The chlorine was well endowed to cause great pain and death but death only occurred in a very small percentage of cases: but damn it all, the suffering was bad enough. Damage to eyes, nose and lungs were ingredients for an easy fight as the sods from Germany saw it. I heard someone say, just a week after the incident at Ypres, that any prolonged exposure to the high concentrates could kill you through asphyxiation. At first he didn't know what asphyxiation meant for he was not a man well tutored in the language of the king, but he was a quick learner. Once he knew the meaning to the word he couldn't stop using it. It was as though he was a fool yesterday and a scholar today. But I tell you this, throw away the damn books and other articles written on the gas because you only need to be scared out of you mind, clawing in the bottom of the trenches to try and hide from the menacing cloud as it approaches, to be killed by it; for exposure over just a few minutes is enough to kill any man: and who wasn't scared of the gas as it clawed its way towards you in a menacing cloud. Oh, sure, when we first saw the cloud we thought little for old habits die hard and the image initially cast upon the mind is that it is a smoke screen, but I tell you this, if we had known of the dangers then we would have been running up behind the French who had several days head start and then overtake them all, just to get away from the affected area.

Pray to God that the wind changes soon.

It is nice to hear the officers and generals give advice as learnt from testing, that to remain at your post was better than to run, for when you ran you breathed hardy and drew the gas into your lungs. Less damage was said to affect those that remained standing in the trench or even sitting upon the edge of the parapet. What was this; it seems that the sod from across no-man's-land has come to join the allies; a spy in officer's clothing. What damn fool would be game enough to sit upon his parapet when the heaviest danger of all was exposure to sniper fire? Or can you convince a man to stand-to in his trench to fight of the damn sods as they come upon you in their thousands with artillery fire as support, which softened up the trenches as the gas came rolling over the flat plains of the Ypres battlefield. Maybe in another place; maybe at another time; but certainly not at a time when one is exposed to immoral weaponry and has no knowledge of it other than the death it causes.

But it is a lesson to be learnt for the future, to sit tight and breathe easily, to stand your ground and allow to gas to flow over you as it continues on with the wind to pass you by. Damn fools; they're all full of advice. Every single man here wants to do his duty but it gets rather hard, sometimes.

That greenish-yellow cloud [and with this the colour seems to change from time to time as though it has something to do with the sky or the sun; I do not know] of death had its moments for the sod, but it probably wasn't as effective as the Germans would have hoped. There were soon many counter-measures one could use against a gas attack, and you could see the damn stuff rolling towards when an attack was in progress, so it wasn't as though you had no warning. It was easy to detect by smell, which was useful if you ended up in a trench which had been exposed to chlorine gas for its residue might linger around for some time after it being employed.

After the war I was always reminded ot the gas attacks whenever I saw a bank of fog early in the morning. I could see the dead, recall the horror. But I was not alone.

It didn't take long for counter-measures to be pulled into place although it was more of a command issued, for orders had to flow from top to bottom and as any soldier will tell you that that can make the difference between life and death as the counter attacks upon the breaches at Ypres had shown.

It is needless for me to say that the sod were all issued with some form of mask, and from what I know, which is usually limited, or has changed so much in its description as it was passed by word-of-mouth, that they had small gauze pads of cotton which were moistened with a bicarbonate solution to either dampen the effects of the gas or null it completely. The German high ranks didn't seem to care about the thousands killed during their wave attacks so why would they care about a few soldiers going through the trauma of inhaling poison gas? This I learnt much later on in the war for our initial counter-measures seemed to be a little cruder but otherwise effective: though in heavy concentrations of the gas it was inevitable that we would suffer in some way.

I hate talking about the gas attacks; it chills me to the bone, so you'll excuse me if I refrain from too much deliberation.

And so the Germans have launched another attack commencing with artillery at 0300hrs, and yes, the gas was amongst the shells delivered. It was directed at the Belgians that existed upon the line. They were exemplary in their will to hold their ground and try to out-manoeuvre the sod by trying to outflank him.

At 0400hrs further gas was release from the ground and the attack fell upon the salient, and although there was fear of the gas the strength of the men's calibre held strong, for there was little surprise in anything the sod carried out this day.

Ample enough water buckets and handkerchiefs were often enough to ward off the worse of the effects of the gas attack as the Germans, ten minutes later, came pouring out of their trenches, but where the gas came rolling over the ground in its thickest the torture of its effects upon men was most profound. And it is here that bravery cast its beautiful head amongst the ugly caricature of the sod, for many men amongst the Canadians knew that they were going to die but stood their ground to kill as many Germans as they could, to give their deaths good cause, to provide their mates with that support in warfare which matters the most. The Germans were so packed together in mass, so confident of their superiority that it was to become their undoing. Yes, the gas will do its duty, many soldiers will retreat as before, and the French… pitiful they are. But the Germans failed to count on the true character of good men willing to sacrifice themselves for such great cause. With little to no artillery support of the ridiculous Ross rifle, the Canadians put a stop to the German advance upon them.

As I have mentioned before I indicated the poor quality of the Ross. They continued to jam all along the line and at a time of great need. Here were the Germans in mass and rapid fire was required. Men didn't have time to kick the bolt back with the heel of their boot, or to hit it back with the entrenching tool, so Lee Enfields were taken from corpses here and there. Some men even procured them permanently to replace the Ross, and where offices scrutinized heavily the absconding of the weapon men were forced to choose to carry both; their Ross in order to keep the officers happy, and the Lee Enfield to keep them safe from harm. There was also a great reliance upon sheer infantry skill at arms and the general use of the machinegun and bayonet. Yes indeed, the bayonet; one of the many pride and joys of the BEF and its supporters; but such a shame that the enemy were too cowardly to come close enough to be skewered by our sheer audacity.

All day long the sod would attack and then retreat; attack and fall back; attack and cower away. When would they learn? It was easier to teach an old dog a new trick.

And when the sun goes down we shall remember them, with their tails between their legs as they scarper away to the reasonable assurance and safety of their trenches: until the morning.

25th APRIL 1915

And the morning comes soon enough. It is 0330hrs in the morning and there is a huge amount of confusion. I shall tell you what I learnt, not of what I knew, for if I told you simply of what I knew then it would be a very short story.

Zero hour had been planned for 0330hrs whereupon all those battalions of hardened men beneath the officer Hull were to perform in a counterattack upon the enemy, to take back from the stinking sod both Kitchener's Wood and St. Julien. And how many battalions did Hull have? Why, ten. How many were to be in the assault? Why, five, of course. I heard that the other five battalions were doing other duties somewhere else either on or behind the line, and/or simply didn't receive orders in time to come to the party: and how lucky they were.

0330hrs and we were still not yet in position, and so Hull delayed the hour of the attack by two hours but someone had forgotten to give word to all of the artillery. What was supposed to be an attack by night ended up being an attack by day, and the sod was given plenty of warning – as though they needed any – and a gift. The gift was our lives.

The Canadian and British artillery that were so ill-informed that they opened up at 0330hrs as advised, but not only did they commence preparatory but several units fired upon St. Julien itself. This would normally not have been a great issue but today it brought much regret. It had been reported that 200 men were still amongst the ruins and that we were not to fire upon it, so of course, not only were our artillery firing upon our own men but at the same instant we were signalling to the Germans that the town was empty of allied troops, henceforth the sod entered the town, killed what little resistance might have been left, and set up machine guns to cover the killing ground in which we were to cross in daylight. It was also a great opportunity for enemy snipers to set themselves up for a smorgasbord of human flesh.

As well as bad fortune there was a little good. Canadian artillery, unknowingly but advantageously, cut to pieces a German assault that was preparing itself at Kitchener's wood to attack the allied line. This is the only good news I could see from any which direction I cared to look for zero hour was upon us and we commenced to move forward, the artillery exceedingly good but low on ammunition.

As for the weather; what can I say? It was raining hard and there was a mist that lay thick upon the ground and in the air. If nothing else it should afford a little cover, and also prevent us from easily seeing any landmarks for reference in our movement forward.

Hull had set up his battalions so that the 1st and 2nd Royal Dublin Fusiliers were facing St. Julien on the right of the line, and the 2nd Seaforth Highlanders and 1st Royal Warwickshire facing Kitchener's Wood on the left of the line. The 7th Argyll and Sutherland Highlanders was in support directly behind those on the left of the line.

The whistle blows and we move forward, weapons at the ready, at the hip, or held across the body: each to his own. The rain has stopped but the mist is still around, but there is not enough of it. Snipers open up upon us immediately and men start to fall, the machine guns commence soon after and the misery is heaping up as though dung upon a mound. Bullets whiz and crack-thump from buildings and long grass. Wherever it is that snipers hide, they shoot to kill, and do well at their primary function. They are disciplines individuals that account for many deaths in the first few minutes of the attack across the flat plains of Flanders. Our advance holds strong; for we are as disciplined, if not more so than the stinking snipers hiding like cowards and shooting us down, but I must remember that we too have our own snipers who perform the same task so wonderfully.

Our objectives are one mile to our front and we maintain good direction in the face of murderous fire, but the murderous fire is about to become a lot worse.

We are dealing with the sniper fire, and now dealing with the machine gun fire; but it is hard to also deal with the further, additional machine gun fire which now comes at us from just south of Kitchener's Wood and Juliet Farm. We are seemingly caught in enfilade, crossing fire. There is no way out of it but straight ahead, to literally walk through the wall of fire from all machine guns which cross our path. It is impossible to believe that we can live through this hell fire being poured down upon us; it is beyond horrific; it is beyond insane; it is not human.

We are now rushing forward in groups, taking bounds as best we can, and as I move forward I looked both left and right. I see hundreds and hundreds of my comrades lying down. I think this is good for they must be pouring fire in upon the enemy, covering their mates so that we can gain ground upon the objectives, and then the reality of it all sinks in. they are not laying down, putting in covering fire; they are all dead. Dead to a man and in what looks like straight lines. The walls of machine gun fire have put a stop to many, but the others, including myself, continue on. I cannot believe it. I look again, this time to the right as I take temporary cover. Ten men are rushing forward and then they hit the ground. It seems so uniform; appears so on-purpose; but it isn't; they too are all dead. I get up and move forward some more, I see men coming along with me but the gaps between us has grown. I feel sick in the stomach; I feel like crying; but the adrenalin in my body prevents me from considering the alternatives to doing my duty. We have lost almost half our men and yet we continue forward and the machine gun fire is not abating.

Suddenly I see a signal. A corporal with more guts than garters is telling us all to get down. I see beyond him some men trying to make a break for it by retreating but they have second thoughts. We all lie down then and get out our entrenching tools. We dig for our lives, and if I hadn't an entrenching tool then I'd be used my teeth and nails. A young boy appears beside me. He's crying and shit scared. He has dropped beside me because he didn't want to be alone in death. He sought me out because all those around him had been shredded to pieces by bullets.

I can hear men, just barely, screaming over the noise of battle to comrades. They get together in their small groups and dig, dig, dig. They scrape hollows within the ground to get away from the murderous fire. The boy beside me is looking at me from time to time and so I give him encouragement. I tell him we'll be okay and that help will comes when the reserves are let loose and when the artillery targets the enemy machine guns; but I don't believe it myself. I shall fight to the death but I know I shall die. No man can live through this.

In other places, so I later learnt, they continue on into the fray. They barely survived.

It was sometime before we got our courage up again and every now and again small groups tried to push forward but the going was too hard. No sooner did you show your untidy little head and the gunners were upon you as fast as the snipers.

The officers were the hardest hit for they were all advancing at the front of their battalions, companies and platoons. So now it is the corporals and sergeants that perform miraculously, with such bravery and great courage that it is hard to believe men can have such steadfast character and will power.

The 7th Argyll and Sutherland Highlanders came in to support those to their front, we, the Dublin Fusiliers had little aid. Nevertheless, the 7th Argyll and Sutherland Highlanders was decimated as those before them. None of us had come close to encountering the sod with bullet, let along our bayonets, and we were only a few hundred yards from our objective.

Later still and two fresh battalions arrived upon the scene. They too were sacrificed for no reason at all, and by 0700hrs we commenced to withdraw and crawl our way backs to the rear as best we could. We can praise the artillery for allowing us to live to fight another day but that can't be said for more than half of us. Not including the battalion sent in to give us aid we had lost 73 officers and 2,346 other ranks.

We had been annihilated, but do you know what was to become of us. We were to be put back into the fight, burdened with fighting in the battle of Frezenberg and Bellewaarde over the next four weeks.

And where were the French. I do not know. Maybe they'd been pinned down somewhere because we saw and heard little fighting from them.

But the day was not over yet for at 1830hrs there was to be another effort made against the Germans gains. The French were requested, rather caudally I would presume, to give aid to the Turcos, a unit made up of Africans, along with the Indian Division. The Turcos did not last long and were last seen fleeing to the rear yelling out 'gas, gas' as they ran. There were wild stories floating around after that, that the Turcos had fled back over the canal and were raping nurses and shooting officers trying to prevent them from withdrawing; chasseurs were even called in to help restore order. But I shall refrain from making further comment. It is also at around this time that Smith-Dorrien was ordered to stand down and hand control of all his men to Plumer. I too shall refrain from making any further comment, for I have already advised you how I felt about that good man, full of good, strategic knowledge.

The only good fortune for us was the fact that by the end of this day enough reinforcements had arrived that it appeared impossible for the sod to expel us from the salient. New lines had been drawn but battles would be waged to alter them further, and they would never be the same as before.

28th APRIL 1915

Today was the day that Smith-Dorrien received the ironic conclusion that he'd not deserved his sacking, for Plumer was given advice on the withdrawal of his troops, a withdrawal which Smith-Dorrien had begged for. Plumer was to be withdraw back to a position that very night as previously suggested by Smith-Dorrien, and so it would seem that we have lost a good commander in Sir Horace, all for the sake of the commander above him [French] to carry out actions which undoubtedly relieved the jealousy he was feeling towards the Horse. It is a pity; no; it is a dying shame that men's lives are treated so poorly because actions just as the relinquishing of commanders for no good reason other than overpowering spite were being carried out. It is however a little rewarding to hear that French was accosted slightly by Foch [his boss] who refused French the option of withdrawal over the option of conducting further counterattacks over the next few days.

It is true to say however that Plumer was also disgusted by the way in which Smith-Dorrien had been treated. Plumer's orders for the withdrawal were no different than what would have occurred had Smith-Dorrien's appeal fell upon open ears, but French, for all intents and purposes, appeared to be nothing less than a death mute, and no pun of any description is intended here for those poor brethren that are born handicapped, for I fight for them as well as I fight for my own.

Oh, dear; it does seem that the higher up you climb the ladder in rank the harder it is to find men of great calibre, but maybe we all consider this the way for we are the ones who live with mud and faeces up to our armpits and with lice in every hem of our clothing.

The main withdrawal, when it finally came, was on the night of the 3rd of May, concluded by sunrise on the 4th, even though some portions of the line were moved rearward on the night previous to this. So here we have Sir Horace, relieved of command for no good reason and French and Foch both finally seeing, one way or another, that he be right in his ideas for the sake of his men and the good of his country. Just how many lives could have been saved from wanton destruction we shall never know?

4th MAY 1915

The withdrawal is complete but Ypres still stands within the protection of men, a semicircle of defence around the entire town, the salient reduced in size but still very much in allied hands. Being approximately three miles shorter in length meant that fewer men were required to defend it. It was a relief to all of those involved and I shall never forget the decimation of our good units which were flung in front of the murderous fire in an attempt to take back what we had lost; but I also feel as though we have been unjustly deprived the company of our comrades deceased for we ended up withdrawing in any case.

War… the stupidity of it will boggle our minds for eternity but we shall still be faced with sending men to their deaths, and why is this? Because there will always be mad men in the world that others are too scared to stand up to.

At 1000hrs the Battle of Saint Julien was officially over.

Two further actions in the beginning of May gave that month something to remember it by. Firstly we saw that Smith-Dorrien was sent home and was never to be awarded a command again. Secondly, the Lusitania was sunk on the 7th May 1915 by a German U-boat. This flung the Americans into the war, for the unnecessary and obvious murder of 1,198 civilians could not be accepted and would be retaliated. The only question now is how long will it take for the Americans to send ground troops into the trenches?

8th MAY 1915

We are at the Battle of Frezenberg which concludes on the 13th of May. There is little to note of our combined efforts to deflect the enemy advance and skew it into oblivion; all I can offer is that the 10th brigade, of which I belonged, proved once more its stubbornness to be moved. Again we fought heroically and conducted out counterattacks as ordered. We seem to be good at what we do, possibly too good, for if we faltered somewhere within the requirements of an infantry soldier then maybe, just maybe, the higher ranks might consider throwing someone else at the line. But we never shirked our responsibility.

On the 10th May the sod released more gas upon the trenches but this had little effect upon us. The cloud was not as thick, it was in smaller pockets as compared to previous attacks, and we had counter measures to put into place which seemed to help where the gas was not too dense.

I would like to also advise you that at some time during my four [plus] years of service in the trenches I was wounded once by the gas which saw me issued with blighty leave, however, the custodian of my word and history [the author of this work] does not know the date of my injury and so he has failed to reflect upon it. This cannot be helped and I know you would love to hear about my withdrawal to RAP, to hospital, and then home, I cannot tell it to you. Neither can I shed further light on my coming together with my new family. I shall tell you this, and this is all I can manage. Before returning to the front I was able to be with my wife and she fell pregnant once more. I was now more determined than ever to come back home in one piece but had to maintain the view that I was dead already in order to accept death and not to lower the morale of the men around me if I should pass into the forever night. The custodian of my memory is making allowances and guessing that I shall be wounded on the 24th May and you shall find out soon enough why; I was on blighty for as few as three weeks.

But back to the reality that is war. The sod had pushed us back 2000 yards and so I must assume that the gas and their artillery were doing the work of their soldiers, for the conscript was no match for our good training.

The idea that the sod held better artillery and more ammunition in which to fire at us was not easy to swallow but the fault of the issue lies with the English Governments inability to manufacture all we needed. The sheer lack of ammunition was seeing to it that we could not match, round for round, the German onslaught, but this was about to change for the better.

Several points need to be clarified here. The men who were set to work in places such as the munitions factories and coal mines were being swallowed up by the military to replace the fallen within the trenches and to strengthen the front as a whole by increasing the number of battalions, brigades and divisions as a whole. Having factories and mines alone does not help if there is no one to work them.

It is here that we see David Lloyd George being made the Minister of Munitions and a good choice he was. It is thanks to him and the woman of our great nation that we would soon see the new appointment pay hugely in our favour.

The German idea that they had artillery superiority was about to be turned upon its head and it would not be long now before the tables would be turned.

24th MAY 1915

This was a terrible day for the 2nd Royal Dublin Fusiliers; the Battle of Bellewaarde which lasted but two days. We had been decimated as it was on the lead up to this day, being cut down maliciously on the 25th April, but today was to prove to be even worse.

The Germans were not about to give up on their efforts in taken Ypres, in particular where it appeared to them that they had come so close to completing their task. It must have seemed an extreme amount of bad luck had befallen them and so they tried once more.

The entire line was well prepared for the onslaught and when it came it came as expected. The sod released a heavy gas cloud of chlorine at 0245hrs which extended for approximately four and a half miles. Behind this the sodding infantry followed with their respirators in place here and there and full of confidence but caution. Along with the artillery and gas the Germans did well to take and capture a few key areas upon the ground, namely Mouse Trap Farm and Bellewaarde Ridge on which the attack was named.

The attack lasted all day and although the sod was cut to pieces in many places they appeared to do more damage to us than we did to them. Ypres was also dealt a miserable hand and practically ploughed flat by artillery from the ground on which it stood.

Nearer St. Julien I was doing my duty as others were doing around me. We had been cut to around half our strength but continued on. We were flanked by another of the 10th and felt comfortable with the support but plainly disheartened by previous losses. It was then that the gas hit us and hit us hard. It seemed to me that the cotton masks we had been issued were cruder than first considered and we succumbed to the terrible uncertainty of what life was like with a lungful of gas. We suffered greatly; too great to honestly fathom.

By last light we were just one officer and 20 other ranks remaining fit for full duty; 645 others were dead, wounded, or missing beneath the great piles of earth which had rained from the sky due to German artillery. It was a most horrid day but the 2nd Royal Dublin Fusiliers would return to continue the fighting. Many of those wounded suffered badly, as bad as any other man drawing in a lungful of gas. It took many men several years to die; others lived in poor health for the remainder of their lives. I would return.

Some good did come of the Second Battle of Ypres, and some bad points always remembered. A system of gas alert and readiness was devised by alarms, masks, and gas-proof shelters, all of which reduced the impact of the chlorine. Our generals woke up to the fact that the French could not be relied upon for they failed to give aid where aid was required, their lack of support in the attack, defence, and counterattack taken to heart. And commanders in general continued to put us in harm's way by insisting we do the impossible; henceforth we were often stunned hard by outrageous losses and little reward. It would be at least two more years before we started to see the light at the end of the tunnel.

6 July 1915

I received a letter from my wife of ten months. It was actually longer than that but I didn't count the time spent in the trenches. For all I was concerned I had experienced ten months of married life and therefore that was all that mattered.

The letter was dated sometime in June, but the letter had gotten wet and some of it was illegible, but in it she expressed all that a good wife does along with much news on the home-front. It appeared that the Daily Mail had written an article and had placed this in their newspaper. It was to request that every single woman who could possibly give aid by manufacturing cotton pads should do so, these could then be employed by the boys on the front. I tell you, she was none too pleased to hear what the sod was doing to us, and all over the wording of policies so decreed by the Hague Treaty of 1899. I'd never heard of the Hague Treaty until advised by her, something she'd read, somewhere, but much talk on the subject came to air over the news for the immoral way in which Germany went about carrying out its hostile actions against us. The response was staggering; over a million pads were made in a day and shipped along with motorcycle goggles made available to protect our eyes. Don't you just love the heck out of those beautiful British Women; God bless every single one? It broke our hearts to learn that the design was, unfortunately, rather useless, for the design in the newspaper was not the best and actually went as far as causing suffocation when wet and the entire idea behind the cotton pads was for them the be wetted with a solution to help protect us against chlorine gas. Many men died because of this but I refrained from saying anything to her about it. Besides, by July six we were all issued with a supposedly well-designed respirator which consisted of a flannel bag which had a small window in the front, a window made of celluloid. The disappointing truth and reality was that the windows were very small and more often than not fogged over, accommodated for by our breathing: what audacity, for us to breathe. Amongst other things they became very hot, very quickly. The entire thing could be pulled over the head. Wherever I went from that day forth I carried it upon my head, except in winter when more efficient means to keep my head warm required I carry it elsewhere. We even had a standing order which told use where to carry it so that if you died and another guy needed it because his was shot to hell then he could help himself to yours, and why not, the Canadians did the same with their Ross Rifles, throwing them aside for a Lee Enfield when one could be appropriated.

Many changes were seen from that day however, for with the introduction of means to counteract the gas became more efficient methods along with other poison gases to counteract the defences. It was also no surprise that the allies were quick, not only to condemn the use of poison gas as employed by the sods, but to hit back with a measured response by creating its own gas capabilities. We had every right.

And so I have seen more than 12 months of fighting, and having returned from being wounded the trenches look the same as they always did. I shall now have to get used to the poor conditions of living in the trenches once more, the softness of my bed at home to be forgotten for quite some time to come.

But what did it mean to live in the trenches? I have tried with little effort to give you an idea but I shall now draw further light onto the subject for your benefit.

I have passed minor word on the sequence of stand-to earlier on, but now I shall discuss it in depth. Everyone in the trenches was required to be up and ready for an impending attack prior to first light. This period of transition was known as stand-to and carried out in total silence with guns and weapons manned, periscopes at the ready and positions maintained. With an uneventful morning and drawing in a brief breath of relief we would breakfast, clean weapons, and carry out menial tasks such as teeth cleaning, toileting and shaving.

Company commanders and RSMs would pass any untoward task onto company captains and CSMs who in turn would pass information onto Sergeants and corporals; LCPLs might then get to flex their muscle and privates would run around carrying out the chores assigned them. But not all chores [or work parties for a better word] were handed down from so high. Platoon sergeants wore their rank because they were thinkers, able to administer a platoon and the men within it; they rarely required the CSM to go ramming his pace stick in every crevice to gain attention for tasks to be passed.

Much maintenance was carried out during the day but only within the safety on the trench system; any work that required doing which existed on top, our front, or just behind the parapet, trench, or bunker, was normally seen to by night when it was hardest to see their movement, but a single sound would bring machine gun fire to rain down upon you. It was therefore customary for many ruses to be performed in order to drain away the noise of wire being erected or a new trench system to be dug down nearer no-man's land than was preferred.

Sentry duty was also rostered within sections and or platoons, to listen and watch for any sign of enemy assault: anything out of the ordinary reported to the nearest NCO or officer.

Late evening was a time for replenishing supplies, bringing up fresh troops, rations, field equipment, and the forever sought relief, but not before another stand-to as dusk turned into night. And the idea of bringing hot food up from the rear was because we weren't supposed to cook it in the trenches for signalling the enemy our position, disposition, or mental state. I guess the simple smell of food was harder to pinpoint but smoke from a small fire drew much attention. A few bombs and machine gun bursts often spoiled a good hearty meal with dirt and crap flying everywhere. Rations were also brought up in either sandbags or hayboxes.

Reliefs were brought forward via the myriad of trenches. You had the 'fire trench' [or fighting/front], the 'support trench', and of course the 'reserve trench'. Each depth trench varied in depth but around six feet will suffice for this explanation, the fighting trench being the deepest at around 12 feet, often the floor of which was covered in duckboards, sandbags, or had firing steps inside – water was forever a problem in the bottom of trenches, in particular where the water table was high, and where there was no water there was mud. I'm sure that from time to time, in particular during the summer months, that there was little to no water or mud but the mind seems to remember the worst of the trench conditions and the more savoury of human souls. If you were to ask me if I remembered Bob I'd say, of course I do, always handy with a joke he was. But if you were to ask me about the trench I occupied on a daily basis I would call it a stinking mud hole in which it would be easy to drown.

Trenches were dug into the ground in a zigzag formation, each length on average being ten yards long, so that is a bomb dropped on your head the blast area was limited by the trenches length: I guess it also prevented your body parts from being blown too far away so your mates could pick up after you, but the job of picking up body litter was not pleasant at all. The lips of the trenches were also built up to help protect against bombs and artillery. The front you should know by now is called the parapet, but the rear was known as the parados. One guy I knew liked to call it paradise instead and said how he'd like to be five miles away from paradise with his feet up. And here's a statistic; it takes six hours for 450 men to dig 275 yards of trench system. You'll notice that I haven't mentioned the casualties within that statistic. Sometimes we were lucky and at others we weren't.

Sleeping conditions, as you can imagine, were not four-star. Officers and senior NCOs had the best of the conditions with small bunkers in which to sleep, eat and give orders, daily pouring over maps and watches, but the poor old infantry private was doused in the misery of sleeping on two feet; with bottom on firing step in the sitting position; or laid back against the turf of a trench which might have half collapsed during a bombardment of the position. The best positions were those upon the duckboards with groundsheet flung beneath to prevent the damp from risen and issuing you with all manner of medical problems from rashes to chilblains.

Relief in place was something that is considered to have occurred, on average, once every eight days but I tell you this, later in the war some men were lucky to see any relief at all. Around 55 per cent of our time was spent within the three trenches on the front, being the fire, support and reserve. The remainder of our time was considered on leave, rest, or training. I can't agree with this however and must insist that time within the first three trenches amounted to at least 65 per cent, and leave in particular was nowhere near as often as it was supposed to have been: leave to the UK was lucky to come around every 16 months or more but was supposed to have been every eight: but it must have been an administrational nightmare to organize leave for so many men on the front. If you work out the mathematics it is staggering. When casualties are suffered; so do the living. I can also tell you the truth of the matter regards time on the line. With the passing of time came an increase in the exposure to combat, for all the regular units.

9th SEPTEMBER 1915

It came to pass that the order banning cameras from the front was given again but this time with more force in the expression and rather severe punishments for breaking the rule. It just wouldn't do for the civilians at home, who made up mothers, sisters and wives of the convicted; and that's what it was to work in the trenches, hard labour if ever it was experienced. Get caught with a VPK in your possession, in particular taking a photo and you were arrested on the spot. Needless to say photos from this day on were far scarcer than any previous period known. You will also be well informed to know that further invasion upon our privacy, which seemed non-existent, fell our way. All of our letters home fell under censorship and went under the prying eyes of those in authority to read our letters. It was a vile war indeed, both at the front and in the rear.

25th SEPTEMBER 1915

Our day of days, the day we opened our doors to gas warfare. Our own batches of chlorine gas had been devised and now ready for delivery upon the debacle known as the Battle of Loos.

I had heard that the code name for the gas was Red Star. I could only hope that this was a fundamental method of ruse to deliver us, and keep from the sods, the use of the gas in order for us all to get our masks on if and when required.

You might image that the front line was extremely long and to expect the sods to employ gas along every square inch was ludicrous, however, best to be safe than sorry and so we were all prepared for whatever might happen. Unfortunately we were met by a greater calamity than any of us could figure.

The barrage of gas cylinders fired from our artillery occurred on a day when the wind was unfavourable and where it didn't linger upon no-man's land like a heavy mist in the streets of London, it drifted back towards us. This was the worst of luck for the prevailing wind of the Western Front was from the west: it was simply unfortunate. Luck would be more with us in the future but today it did not exist. But this wasn't the only bad luck that we suffered for upon the firing line there were numerous canisters which could not be armed due to an uncanny reason: the turning keys which had been provided were incorrect and could not be used. It was as though the gas had a mind of its own and on delivery had decided, most purposely, that a withdrawal or retreat was the best form of attack.

The sods soon carried out a counter barrage and the gas cylinders that sat exposed upon our firing line soon become the target of our greatest despair, the gas erupting in all directions before settling with the wind, lingering around for all to see and breath.

Our own trenches soon became inundated by our own gas and the masks we had sitting upon our heads were brought down over our faces. Some of the men were seen deliberately lifting their masks from place upon them because they could not draw sufficient breath to fight the battle before them and hence they succumbed to one of the worst deaths upon the battlefield.

It was fortunate that the men at home, or even those with the trenches whom had been chemists in their former lives, came up with more advanced methods of counteracting the gas. We had what was known as 'hypo', or Hypo helmet. It was a bag that could be placed over the head, or pulled down over it if worn as a hat. Its fabric had been treated with a chemical known as sodium hyposulfite and the goggles were made of talc and fogged up soon after fitted. The chemical within the fabric also got into our eyes during foul weather which didn't help matters at all. A mouthpiece was added for good measure which allowed for the build-up of carbon dioxide to diffuse correctly. Later versions such as those employed in January of 1916 were treated with hexamethylenetetramine [the PH Helmet] to ward off the devilish phosgene.

25th DECEMBER 1915

It is our second Christmas on the front. To think that it was supposed to be over by Christmas. It's a lesson to be learnt, not to accept optimistic views too readily when coming down from higher for it serves morale a short burst but wears off quickly and is hard to restore. We were also becoming so proficient in the trenches that we seemed accustom to it. How's that; to be accustom to living in such filthy conditions; to be used to seeing men die and their corpses eaten by over-sized rats. How is it we can be accustomed to lice, disease, and the torment of death on a minute-to-minute time frame? It was as though life itself was sheer misery and I tell you now that the suicide rate amongst the men increased for a while there. I saw it with my own eyes but refuse to speak of it, for it isn't nice to see a young man shoot himself in the head due to the insanity of war turning the tide of your mental clarity of thought. I am also forced to recall the Christmas Truce of the previous year but we would have all been hard-pressed to see or hear of another attempt at fraternization with the enemy.

As for the previous year there was no real fighting on the front, no large scale battles fought, no counter attacks to be ensued. It was too cold for that. Maybe I can hear you scoffing at the comment but here's the truth of the matter. How can you fire your rifle when your hands are twice their original size due to frostbite and sheer cold? You might know how it is to try to lift something up on a cold and damp morning at find it impossible to feel what you are doing, ah, ha; you see and understand. Now you times that by ten, or maybe a hundred, for in the bitter cold of Europe, when flesh and bone are exposed to the elements hour after hour and day after day, it becomes a sheer impossibility to even lift your cups canteen to your mouth for a drink of lukewarm tea, and our feet are no better, swollen and suffering severe pain every minute of the day. You cannot fight a battle this way, when it's impossible to walk or crawl; when you can't even pick up an item and not feel it, dropping or spilling whatever it is you try to put into your hands.

Some men were more fortunate than others and by sheer good fortune may have found themselves in BHQ for an hour or more with a message requiring a reply, and during this time you get warm and so when you return to the trenches you are good for another hour or more. You become useful to your mates and help them with a cigarette or possibly a shave. There is never a day goes by that one or more men have to file down the line seeking to bring a little life back into comrades too cold to even scratch themselves. Is it no wonder that these men feel closer to me than a brother or twin?

There is much misery suffered in the trenches to date and there is much more to come, all for a shilling a day. It's ludicrous. There are able-bodied men back in England shirking their responsibilities, thieving money from all around them, lying about their inabilities to fight on the front due to certain illnesses or injuries. It is these same men that seek and steel the medals of others so that they can wear them in later years, pretending to have served overseas. These are the worst kind of men and there are plenty of them in every society.

And before the months of spring are upon us I have the good fortune to come into view of something new. The factories at home are spewing out a new machinegun called the Lewis-gun. It's far easier to carry about, being much lighter and less cumbersome. We are also soon to be introduced to the Stoke Mortar which sounds very reassuring in their funny little way. You feel somewhat... safer, with the sound of such weapons being close at hand.

And so after many weeks of sheer misery in the trenches endured it is time once more to commence for the many battles to come, but one more thing will bring the temptation to cause havoc amongst us all, but we are too proud to allow it to separate us into factions.

The Easter Rising.

Letters were coming from England and Ireland, newspaper articles read out to men in the trenches. Padres got involved to try to simmer our dispositions of mind and generals endeavoured to ensure that no wedge was placed between those fighting on the front. But we were strong of mind and conviction and had made our decisions almost two years before. There would be so sway of mind.

I knew as any other did of the Irish Volunteers, that band of armed men created on the 25th day of November back in 1913, and now of the Easter Rising which lasted for seven days commencing the 30th day of April this year.

Back in Ireland there was seven days of fighting, back here in Flanders we have had our fill with two years of combat and God knows how many more to come.

The Irish Republican Brotherhood [IRB] had created the Irish Volunteers and to tell you the truth it was an insult to what I was trying to achieve; a life for my family which was to be free of fear. Many of us knew, if not all [for we seldom spoke of it], that the IRB was intent upon receiving aid from the sod. In order to do this the IRB must be willing to aid the sod, too. But you won't find a spy of any description in the trenches. Not only is our mail read before being sent home but we don't wish to endanger our own lives of the bitterness felt due to clash of territories or religion by filling them with hate. We had far worse things to bear, such as the frailness of our minds in putting up with the war and our struggle to stay alive. Maybe if the IRB were to experience what we, ourselves, were experiencing, then they would put away their inner ambitions and live in peace, peace as we were fighting for. This stinking IRB was to try and effect a German infiltration from Ireland, to have Irish prisoners of War join together and fight against the English: but they would be fighting against their own as well, for our battalions, regiments and divisions were fighting side by side.

I also heard the rumours of a German boat, disguised as Norwegian, smuggling weapons into Ireland, but this was seized by the Royal Navy.

The Easter Rising is an extensive history in itself, with members and manoeuvres, treachery and sinful reprise, the cause of frustrations and death: frustration being an understatement. It is not for me to here and now go into its detail, but the effect it had upon us good men fighting for a cause. The effect seemed to be slight, if at all. We still fought beside those that might have opposed the IRB, but then again many civilians, who had suffered more deaths than either side within the conflict, turned upon those that might have been considered brethren – or so it seemed. No matter what the IRB have done in the past, present, or future will distract me, nor those fighting at my side, from our true beliefs in who we are and what we are fighting for.

24th JUNE 1916

We have suffered annihilation before and we to face it again. We are now at the Battle of Albert, and many of you will know it as 'Battle of the Somme', and I wish to speak to you about it.

Firstly the Battle of Albert was the opening phase of what was to become the Battle of the Somme. It upsets me sometimes that there is confusion when forgetting about the name Albert, for it is part and parcel of this book's title, in a way: it's all in the picture. I guess you were wondering where it came from. But more on this a little later; for the moment I wish to concentrate upon the Battle of Albert, not the Somme as a whole. Let us reflect on the most heinous time of war other than that experienced at the Third Battle of Ypres; or Passchendaele if you so prefer.

This battle to come was a major insight of those imposing a death sentence upon us for although the idea of making for an historical breakthrough of the enemy lines seemed sound enough there was a lot that went wrong with the thinking of men in power. I have read in history books that the total length of the front to be condemned to the fight to fall upon the BEF was 14 miles, and others offer 18 miles. I have wasted little time on the considerations of this for what matters most to me is the bad memories of death and mutilation; the crying out of strong men now broken calling out for their mothers. It brings a tear to my eye just thinking of it. But for all due purposes in writing this book I have considered the frontage which the BEF be directly responsible for, to be 18 miles.

Zero hour for the operation was not advised us. It was a secret. But on this day in 1916 a bombardment commenced which could be heard from many places in England along and near the coast and supposedly up to almost 300 miles away, 1.7 million shells in all, if not more, in predatory fire over the duration of the week. This is how; it did not stop for 80 minutes and continued for seven days: it was to be a ruse of which I shall explain. This was the opening stages of the Big Push. After the main bulk of aggressive firing the guns would continue but at a slower rate and by night half of them would cease. The machine guns would then open up during the night until morning, cutting off resupply in the rear. All guns would then open up with another 80 minute barrage followed by slower rate for the remainder of the day, and so forth.

Consider this if you will, for visual affect only; there was an artillery piece or mortar placed at every 17 yards apart for 18 miles firing non-stop for 80 minutes, it is understandable therefore that little ground would go unscathed. We would hit the sod where it hurt; kill them, maim, them, shatter their courage and turn them into dribbling idiots. We would smash their shelters and trenches, smash their fire fortifications, and smash their will to live. But it didn't turn out that way. It was to be the end of the colour of nature, the poppies, yellow tansy and marguerites being obliterated from the scene, and that were about the strength of it all. More artillery ammunition fired in the week as compared to that fired during the first 12 months of war, all for the sake of killing our only current joy; the colour of the flowers around.

I hear you ask the obvious and so I shall now reveal the ruse. For seven days the enemy were hit with 80 minutes of fire. On the morning of the attack they would receive 65 minutes before we pushed out from our trenches and prepared for our advance upon the presumed, broken line, the enemy expecting a further 15 minutes of firing. There was one major disappointment in the firing however; one third of all shells were duds.

An important aspect in the lead up to the attack was the question of what damage the bombardment was having on the German defences and the units which opposed us. Information on the different units was rather important for some were gutsier than others, some loaning to fear and cowardice more readily than another, and some willing to fight to the death for their flag.

Raiding was always a prompted move and each major unit on the line, being a division, was to conduct at least one raid per night to gather as much information as possible on the subjects of enemy strength, weapons, logistic support, units, possible tactics, equipment, enemy habits, his intensions, and morale. Morale was extremely important and prisoners never went unquestioned, and were very useful.

Raids were many and varied in size from a half-platoon size raid to one being a full company in strength; there were also casualties to be faced for it was rare that a raid was conducted without someone getting a bullet or bayonet in the gut, and not every raid reached its destination, for some raids had been gunned down before reaching the objective and had to crawl back to the line in retreat.

Now, having told you that the information was invaluable you would consider it to be taken in and adhered to for all intents and purposes, to aid the assault to come. But no matter how often a returning raid would report that the wire in front of the enemy was not being cut and destroyed as expected, it would not be believe. Some may have even considered such a lame report as blasphemous and beyond exaggeration.

26th JUNE 1916

It would seem like any other day; apart from the barrage taking place; but something different was in the air today.

The RFC had a total of 185 planes in ten squadrons against the sod who held just 129. It gave us air superiority. Air superiority meant that the sod was unable to see from above the battalions, regiments and divisions moving into positions behind the lines in readiness for the main attack to come and later refused them the information of the huge numbers of cavalry preparing to unleash hell [which never dawned] later on. Try as the sod might to gain information or even conduct artillery registration from their balloons, of which we had 16 in the air, they could do little against us. It was easy to distinguish the English balloons from the sodding ones; ours were grey and theirs were black.

And so I looked up into the sky one bright morning to be confronted by no less than six of our aircraft drawing upon some enemy [around four]. At 8,000 feet it looked spectacular and one can be forgiven to forget the war to their front for a few minutes as one English lad dove down from high above and chased a German towards a fast-approaching ground, turning at the last minute with the English hot on his tail, firing his machine gun with great expertise. Here they flipped and flopped, drawing closer to the crowd of onlookers as we peered up from the trenches, seeing the live show which was mesmerising in every detail. It was hard to believe that a flying machine could manoeuvre in the way the pilots handled them. Loop the loop, twist and turn, the English plane was joined by another and then the sod had no chance at all and was hit by some fire from their guns, and whether or not the sod was hit directly or not he failed to bail out and the plane screamed down towards the earth with a little smoke coming from behind. He managed to pull his plane up a little and it seemed to skid over the top of a copse of trees before slamming into the earth and bursting into flames. It was a marvellous sight and yells of joy erupted from the men all around, and then a sniper from the enemy trenches shot dead a man exposing too much of himself above the trench. Suddenly a single German plane gets through and starts shooting his machine gun at a balloon of ours which is registering targets. He passes and then turns to give it another try. Then I can see two dots in the sky as the men jump from the balloon and parachute to safety with the sod trying again and again to see the balloon engulfed in flames but it did not happen, and then he was chased off by several English and I don't know what happened then because they disappeared from sight. It would seem for all intents and purposes that we had the upper hand, but the sod held the higher ground and looked down upon us, seeing far more of us than we could of them. Each German individual could see far more of no-man's land than we could, and that would account for something when the attack started. The Germans also did one other thing of mischief. They realized how ridiculous it was to fire their artillery in retaliation against our counter battery fire, our balloons and aircraft, and so put them to silence. We naturally believed the Germans to be light on guns and briefed a sigh of relief in the thought that the attack would be all the easier when it arrived. It was just another insecurity to be dealt with later.

27th JUNE 1916

Whilst helping a wounded mate to the rear I came across some men on horseback and enquiring as to whether or not they could help us by providing us a ride; they said that they couldn't as they were going in another direction and were not to delay their orders. They did manage to give slip some information which my later forages in the pages of history proved to be quite correct; future orders would also reveal much of the plan of attack upon the enemy trenches and towns beyond and I shall now reveal some of this to you.

The first day of the offensive to come was made up solely of the men of Great Britain and Ireland and Lord Kitchener's New Army, along with small units from Bermuda and Newfoundland. Canadians, ANZACs and South Africans were not present on the first day as many were on leave in England or at rest behind the lines.

Three cavalry divisions were to be employed to roll up the flanks in the rear once the enemy positions to the front had been breached, but this never eventuated, but this is not to say that an opportunity was not made available, for it was, but the poor reflection of strategy within the eye of our commanders above refused to unleash them of their bonds behind our front line.

There were three lines of enemy trenches that needed to be cleared before sighting the villages and towns beyond, the main road between Amiens and Bapaume [Albert being almost central along this line; approx 16 miles from Amiens and nine from Bapaume], being the centre line for our advance. We had also known for some time of the Russians and their efforts to push upon the Germans in the east, this came on the 4th day of June and hence the sod was forced to endure cutbacks in their strength managing the defences along the Somme. This appeared to give us the upper hand but was an illusion.

I now think it is time to reflect upon Albert and in particular the cathedral there. The town was to change hands during the very early stages of the war and also later on, but seemed to spend most of its time within the hands of the allies [possibly an optimistic view]; so close was it to the fighting that all of its citizens had left with everything they could cart or carry, even so, the Germans still held the high ground but the allies held the tower of the cathedral from which to exercise their right in registering artillery targets and their adjustments upon other targets of choice. It was during the early days of the war that Germans tried all they could to see the tower brought down by artillery fire, for the idea of having artillery spotters employ it as the great vantage point it was, was simply too much to ignore. The sodding bastard eventually hit the tower on which stood a marvellous statue of the Virgin Mary but the French engineers took measure to ensure she didn't fall and fixed it into position with lengths of thick and heavy cables.

It boggles the mind to consider why the French went to such great measures to ensure the Virgin stood her ground, even if on an angle, for a legend rose at around that time, in particular amongst French troops, that the war would not finish until the statue fell. I can only presume therefore that the French considered the felling of the statue as a German victory to come. As time went by we English also took up the visualized belief that should she fall the war would end. There seemed to be much confusion in this however for I have heard many versions of the same tale and many of those are that whoever should knock it down would lose the war. So if the Germans knocked it down then we would obviously win. But how did this all come about.

Hundreds of thousands of troops passed through and near, or past, the tower, and the Virgin upon it was quite easy to see and from quite some distance. There was within it a mystique and symbolism; strong belief and understanding. Both sides in this war believed in God. Inside the German prayer book found in the trenches was the picture of Jesus looking down upon a German soldier who had just been killed; an almost identical picture can be found in our [allied] field prayer book: obviously the soldier looks different and wears a different uniform. The words in each mean the same, for in both books can be read the words, With Jesus in the Field. How can this be? It would seem that both sides idolised the statue of the Virgin Mary, and inexplicably for many reasons both sides more or less believed in the same legend.

Let me see if I can find something here. It would seem that the Germans believed that whoever knocked down the Virgin would win the war, but many of the sod, in particular after 1916, seemed to believe that whoever knocked her down would be conquered. I say that fear held all, that religion and belief restrained them all from knocking down the Virgin, and for all the truth there was about it only one thing had become clear; when the Virgin fell the war would be over, and neither side wished to lose.

The attack to come was over ground not particularly healthy for those that might, in a hail of bullets, seek to take cover. In most places over the length of the ground to be covered was open and although rich soil was to be found ahead [great for copses and wheat] the ground was of chalk. There were no divots in which to seek cover from fire, between villages and copses [with a few larger woods]: it was open. Cover was what we made of it which brings me to the 'alteration' aspect of what was to come, for we were carrying out extensive mining and the craters created from such would provide a little assurance in regards to the safety of a bare few.

We were advised in time that it was going to be an easy walk over to the enemy trenches, into which we would find ourselves a defeated enemy with hands up in eagerness to surrender, so in order to make great advantage of our gains we were to carry as much equipment as humanly possible with the waves behind the lead being burdened with additional stores such as duck-boards and rolls of barbed wire. It was no easy feat to carry so much.

Bayonet and rifle, the two main weapons of the war; as well as these we carried [which changed widely across the entire front] 150-220 rounds of ammunition, grenades, sandbags, entrenching tools and spades, wire cutters, signal flares [seventy pounds-plus of equipment]. One further item which was new to the front was the steel helmet. It came to be that the steel helmets reduced head casualties by around 75%. All of this was on top of everyday field kit such as belt, water bottle, pouches, groundsheet, haversack, mess-tin, iron rations, socks, two gas masks, mortar bombs, and if you were unlucky, a stretcher or telephone cables. The weight seemed to go up and down like a seesaw and with each different attack and season came different needs and requirements.

Our advance into the enemy trenches was to be conducted in waves with two platoons in each wave [400 yard frontage], two eaves per company, and eight waves per battalion; stretcher bearers and battalion HQ element would bring up the rear. The advance would also be a measured one of around fifty yards per minutes: in other words, extremely slow, too slow in fact for many commanders who chose to alter it as they saw fit prior to entering no-man's land. We were not to run even if fired upon, not unless we were 20yards or less from the enemy, for this was considered unnecessary. The idea of the slow advance was due to the belief that the artillery would have rendered the enemy barbed wire as obliterated and the trenches as empty of opposition: neither was the case. There would be no looking after a wounded comrade, no taking of prisoners, and any man refusing to go over the top would be shot by the Military Police.

The Germans were in hold of the best ground, being higher than ours and therefore dryer due to fewer problems with the water table. Not only were their machinegun positions well-endowed and constructed with concrete and steel, and there were 55 machinegun posts for every mile of front to be assaulted, but their trenches were ten foot deep with extremely elaborate dugouts and command posts dug down forty feet or more with tunnels connected to trenches in several directions. The luxury of each, as we were to learn in the near future, were panelled and well furnished, like barracks rooms for officers back in Berlin, with bunk beds and cupboards, dining tables, chairs and a system of ventilation, all wired up to electricity. It put our own dugouts to great shame. Their reserve and depths trenches were as good as those at the front. Trenches and tunnels lead right up to the villages which sat behind them, the buildings and cellars of the crumbling structures being employed well with the ability to defend. Across the entire frontage of our assault could be found nine major towns so well fortified that you would have to consider them forts of the greatest strength and able to endure great masses of artillery fire with infantry assault supported heavily with tanks, and you'd need engineers in order to help you clear them of all enemy. It is too profound to consider; it appears an almost impossible task when looked back upon. Between the villages where the ground was open and sparse they built other miniature forts to ward off the threat of being flanked.

Haig wanted the attack to take place on the 25th but this was postponed until the 29th and 0730hrs. It was because of the weather; two days of summer storms which made the crossing unfavourable and we needed everything in our favour. And then a bolt of lightning strikes several men dead because all of us in the trenches carry a rifle with a bayonet on its end. Success could not be won on speculated formulations alone, but we did out-number the sod seven to one and with such outstanding superiority it was seen as impossible for us to be defeated in what was to come. We were just shy of 130,000 men [when considering a FULL strength division] to take part in the coming attack, made up with what appeared to be 60% of Kitchener's New Army. We were either regular soldier or volunteers opposing an army made up of mostly conscripts: or so I was lead to believe.

28th JUNE 1916

It was still raining and the time of the attack was scheduled for the morning, and then the news arrived that the attack would be postponed but yet again. We were now set to commence the assault [walkover] at 0750hrs on the 1st of July. The news did not go down well. Tempers were frayed, the weather and conditions were extremely bad, and there was so many men in the trenches that there was hardly room to move. Can you imagine having to stand up all day and all night without sleep for lack of room? We were ready to go, there is no doubt about it. The men were eager to have it over with and the mass graves sat empty behind us ready to be filled. Everything was as well prepared as could possibly be expected, but the poor manufacture of the artillery shells let us down, but maybe the weather had something to do with their poor performance in shredding the wire to our front. Our thoughts were only interrupted here and there with the sound of a single shot being fired far away, a man shooting himself in the leg to get himself away from the war only to find his stretcher being escorted by armed men in readiness for his execution to come.

30th JUNE 1916

The sun had risen and stand-to was over with. I took the opportunity to grab a periscope and to take a look at the enemy trenches and the ground in which we were to cross in the morning. All I could see were the scars upon the ground indicating the enemy trenches and a mist made of dust laying over the entire area, so thick that it was impossible to see through for any great depth. I was amazed that so much dust could be present after so much rain but it is sheer indication as to how hot it can get in Flanders during the height of the summer months. Gone were the colours of the wild flowers; gone were many of the copses.

The big guns had ben firing now for seven days and I knew that the gunners were tired to the bone, hot and bothered, and stripped to the waist due to the hardship of their forte. And so with these images in my mind I try with my entire might to achieve a rest state or even sleep, but the task is not an easy one, not for a single sole in this damn place.

1st JULY 1916

It was 0400hrs and the big day was upon us, and the men prepared as best they could for what lay ahead. Few concerns seemed to appear on faces for we had had it drummed into us how easy it would be with the enemy trenches empty and the sodding reserve too far to do anything about reinforcing the front line, and almost every man to the last was so happy to see an end to the waiting for tonight we might get some descent sleep, but I shall tell you now that only the dead ever gained rest from war.

Our brothers-in-arms, the 1st Royal Dublin Fusiliers, having served in Gallipoli and now serving her on the Somme were to lead the attack in our quarter and I, as a member of the 2nd Royal Dublin Fusiliers were to be their backing, bringing up their rear in what was to be one of our darkest hours. My story of the attack has only just begun but I shall cut to the chase in regards to casualties to put your mind to rest. We went into battle with 23 officers and 480 other ranks, and can you image how many of us came back [remembering of course that little more than 10 per cent of us were now originals]? When the fighting was finished on that first day we were 9 officers and 169 other ranks; everyone else was dead, missing, or wounded: wounded in the sense that they could not carry on but needed full treatment in order to recover from injury. What do you say to that, ah? This damn war was cutting us to pieces, literally.

With the thought that the rain was behind us came a reminder that nature be ever present, for a light rain commenced to fall upon the battle field. Thankfully it didn't last long and before the whistle blew for us to depart the trenches it had ceased.

The shelling continued at the slow rate which we were now quite used to and it wouldn't pick up for a few minutes. It would be then that we could count on 65 minutes of heavy barrage prior to or time of departure falling upon us all. And then it came and scared the hell out of us all. We were all expecting it but it jolted us all the same, more so than any previous day. I think this might have been because today we knew we were going over the top and some of us didn't quite believe the words of the generals that the attack was going to be a piece of cake: it's somewhat strange to see men smiling one moment and then see such smiles fade as the guns blazed away. Something rather peculiar happened then. The sodding artillery opened up and rained down upon us. Guns that had been silent for so long were now hitting back at us in retaliation. It was as though they hadn't been scratched at all and that they knew we were coming; but how could that be possible?

I saw the rum going around for the last time and only a few of us refrained; most partook in quenching the dryness within their throats and picked up a little more courage as the warmth of the rum hit the spot. I saw two men get quite drunk and they were laughing away merrily unto themselves for no one could hear them properly over the noise of the barrage. The sergeant then came and saw to it that no further rum was issued to them and the last dregs in the cups canteen was emptied or given to someone else close by; but it was too late. These two men would meet death as drunk as could possibly be, walking aimlessly into the interlocking fire of German machine guns. No one else did much better mind you, being ordered to walk straight ahead into oblivion and of course obeying the order for fear of the Military Police stationed back in the trenches behind us. And so it was time to exit the trenches and line up, or simply step out in line as the whistle blew, and some of those commanders smart enough to order their men to move to the front of the wire, in front of the trenches, before zero hour in some cases, actually made it to the other side of no-man's land in one piece: all that might be left was to try and come back again later.

I saw some men praying to God before shaking out with the formation and thought it a good idea if I might do the same. What could it hurt to ask for some form of protection in what was about to befall us and not a man amongst us really knew what to expect. If we were to believe the generals then we were in for a grand old day of advancing upon empty trenches, but if we believed our gut then we knew we were in for much trouble and misery. I then said two prayers, one for myself and the other for my family. I never prayed again after that day for quite some time. I then looked up and saw we were ready to take the place of the 1st once they had commenced towards the enemy, and then the ground shook violently. It was the artillery along the entire front of 18 miles, rapid fire from every single gun on the line, mortars included. This was to last for ten minutes.

I was sure as sure could possibly be that no man could survive such intense fire, but there was more to come. After eight minutes of fury the mines that had been dug beneath no-man's land and towards the enemy were blown sky high. We could see great masses of the earth erupt 4,000 feet into the sky and I suffered a great calamity then for the man two down from me was shaking with fear. I could see the horror in his eyes and he seemed lost of conscious thought. I could see that he wanted nothing more than to be with his mother but that was not to be. He would go over the top soon enough and meet his end as many other did that day. Clods of earth then swamped the trenches and some men were wounded bad enough not to take part in the crossing of the fields of fire; those lucky bastards who might lose a finger or suffer the remainder of their lives with a permanent scar across the face from such a deep wound that they couldn't carry on with today's fight.

Ten mines in total were fired [1 at 0720hrs, 8 at 0728hrs, and 1 being ten minutes late], three of these were detonated by use of more than twenty tonnes of explosive, the remainder consisting of around 5,000lbs apiece. It was sheer ear-blowing, the closer you were to one the worse off you were.

Suddenly the barrage stopped. For a few moments everything appeared to be so at peace. There was not a sound to be heard other than a bird in the distance, for even the sods had stopped firing. New targets were then plotted and the artillery engaged these.

And then the whistle blew and the advance across no-man's land commenced at a crawl. This was it, this was the time we had waited for, and then to our flank a German shell made a direct hit within one of the trenches, an entire platoon killed with the blink of an eye. The screams just managed to fall upon my ear as the backs of the 1st were moving away from us and towards the enemy. Officers and other NCO's were eager to get on with the job and words of encouragement fell from their mouths and then the machine guns opened up and the first of many casualties began to fall to the ground as casualties of war.

Bugles were sounding in the German trenches, this could be heard well enough, and I could hazard a guess that the sod would be spilling out of their dugouts in the thousands to man their positions, to join the ranks of the few guns which had opened up, to be joined by many more soon enough.

It wasn't long before the few German guns that had been firing were joined by others and all you could hear from the trench was the noise of the machine guns as they mowed down rank after rank, wave after wave. This chorus of killing was then joined by a few shells from the German artillery which were set upon with counter battery fire. And the machine guns continued without rest to kill and maim; seemingly impossible numbers of men were being hit and when they fell upon the ground hit again to make doubly sure that they were dead.

For all intents and purposes it seemed that the 1st had been decimated to the last man when, at 0900hrs, it was our turn to exit the trenches. Yes, that's correct; there is no calling off an attack when it's in progress. Haig would push on and keep on pushing on until not a man was left to fight this bitter war. And how did I feel to be climbing out of the trenches knowing that death awaited us in no-man's land, for the machine guns hadn't yet turned upon the parapet of the trenches but were seemingly waiting for us to join our fallen comrades in the middle of the killing ground, and the guns did not cease for a seconds respite.

I let my eye sway and saw small clusters of men to both left and right, fallen men bleeding badly and tending themselves as best they could with what dressings they had on them. We were not to stop and give aid, I recalled this, but I felt as though I were cheating them by continuing on into the jaws of death, but continue I did. And as I should look further afield to either flank I could see so few of our men still advancing for we too had been decimated. It was then that a bullet hit my helmet and knocked me to the ground. It knocked me unconscious but I don't know for how long. When I came too, the waves of men were still moving across no-man's land and being killed so that every foot of ground seemed to carry a dead man. The ground was littered with bodies.

I attempted to move and someone fired at me in anger, but again the bullet hit my helmet but this time knocked it clean off. I scurried forward to shallower ground and a machine gun burst almost found me, dirt spraying all over my back as I crawled into safe harbour. I rolled down into the crater and gasped for air before looking around and seeing two badly wounded men and another eight dead.

One of the wounded men, his left arm missing from the elbow down yelled out for me to keep my head down. He said that so earnestly and loudly for he knew that the slightest move would draw machine gun fire to fall upon them and they didn't need that. He was trying to bandage his own arm. I then glanced at the other man but couldn't see his face because it was a mass of flesh and blood. I would learn soon enough that he had lost his nose, right ear and eye, and his jaw had been so badly shattered that it hung in a poor position. His breathing did not sound at all healthy, as though his throat was filled with blood and guts. He was sitting rather still and obviously in great distress and shock.

German artillery then struck our own trenches and no-man's land with great vigour, and this coupled with the machine gun fire made it impossible for any man to make it across to the enemy trenches in our sector.

I then went against the good advice of the wounded man and glanced back towards our own line and could just manage to see another wave of our lads climb out of the trenches and commence the advance, but it took only a few seconds before there was only a few men left to take on the brunt of the German line. I would learn later that in some places they actually made it to the other side and with very few casualties, but it wasn't to be where I was. It was then that I glanced towards the Germans and saw their infantry getting up on to their parapet and shooting at us along with the machine guns, whose task it now seemed to kill us as we poured out of the trenches, the infantrymen with rifle taking down those that survived the initial onslaught. Another burst of fire made me pull my head down.

Oh; how so clear it was that the enemy dugouts were so superior to our own. It was as though they had gone through the week-long bombardment without a scratch. Here we were outnumbering them 7 to 1 and we were being cut down so easily, but the lads carried out their orders and the waves kept advancing. It was clear that I'd only been concussed for two or three minutes.

I removed my pack and took all the field dressings I could to the wounds of the men in my midst, starting with the one with the missing arm. He was drained of energy and purpose but the bleeding was stopped. He commented on how tired he was and he drifted off to sleep as I then attended the other man. I rummaged through some of the dead and took some dressings from them and gave aid as best I could. I tried as best I could to clean the hole where his nose was and had trouble stemming the flow of blood, for it was a task and a half for him to breathe through his shattered jaw which I ended up fixing in place with a barrel bandage and maintained as best I could a gap there for him to breathe through. It seemed like forever but I know that little time had passed.

A harsh yelling and loud voice then hit my ear. From somewhere outside the crater in which I found myself I heard the order to 'Come on! Get up and rush them, lads!' and then an intense amount of machine gun fire ripped through the air as the scream of men trying to rush the enemy were brought to their end. It was then that another wounded man fell into my crater with blood across the entire front of his chest.

I wasted not a single moment this time and ripped his haversack from his back whilst keeping low so as not to be fired upon. I then ripped off his shirt and found a bullet hole in his chest. His breathing was hard and uncomfortable, his teeth gritted together in agony and him being extremely restless from the pain. I assured him as best I could and a bullet almost found its mark but again the new helmet saved the day but was torn from his head leaving a ghastly red and bleeding gash under his chin where the strap had been.

I looked again at the wound and saw one small hole. I put my right hand in behind his back and felt around with my finger tip. I found an exit hole and proceeded immediately to stem the flow from his two holes. I managed as best I could and although he was in horrid pain he seemed to be able to handle being placed upon his right side where his right lung filled with blood but his left remained clear and he was able to breathe with a ghastly sound of gurgling emitting from him. It must have been a horrible time for him, being half drowned in your own blood.

Now it was time to check on my other two patients and I found to my dismay that the man with the shattered jaw was dead. His injuries had been too much for him. The other, with the missing arm, seemed to be in a stable way and so I maintained close visual on the third. It was then that I realised the dilemma we were in. we were stuck three quarters, or there about, of the way across no-man's land and stuck in a crater. There was no getting out of it and therefore my patients would die. What could I do but try and eliminate the threat, and so doing as many were doing along the 18 miles of frontage I took to taking pot shots at the Germans from the edge of the crater in which I found myself, making sure to lift my eye over the parapet of the crater in a different spot each time to avoid being killed. I managed to kill two of the sodding bastards but each time I fired my rifle a machine gun would retaliate by order of someone within their trenches.

I felt like a coward but what good would it do me to try and rush the enemy now. I would be gunned down before I'd gotten six feet, and although I'd managed to get this far into the fight, as the dead and wounded had that were with me, I was no longer flanked by hundreds of men and therefore an easy target. All I could manage to get out of this mess was to try and keep these other two men alive long enough for them to receive proper aid. But I didn't like the chances of the chest wound of getting through the day, let alone the night if this failed attempt at taking the German trenches was to continue past dusk.

We had been here for almost two hours when the man with the chest wound motioned for a drink of water. I wasn't sure if I could give it to him because of his wound and couldn't remember what I was to do. If I gave it to him he might choke and die, I was simply lost for any idea of what to do. And then I recalled that only stomach injuries were not to be given water: but I wasn't one hundred per cent sure. His wound was bandaged well enough, as too was the one with the missing left arm, but I was not a medical officer nor orderly and couldn't be relied upon to give any assurance that my taking sympathy on him might kill him. I chanced to say that I had none to spare and left it at that, but he insisted I search the haversacks and equipment of the dead around us. I therefore had little choice in the matter and did all I could. What little water I did find I gave to him and miraculously enough, after a short choking fit which started his bleeding again, he was brought under control and managed to force a smile upon his face for just a few seconds before remaining still and relatively quiet as he continued with his rasped breathing.

It was well past midday for the sun was high above and the sound of war continued without a break although the sound had abated quite considerably when compared to earlier on. The worst of the killing had been done and I was to learn in later years that 60,000 men to fight this day were casualties, almost 20,000 of which were dead. It was a dark day indeed.

Darker still was what happened next. A German bomb was thrown into our crater, obviously in retaliation for my firing from it. It landed next to the man with the missing arm. We locked eyes, me and him. I was too far from it to pick it up and thrown it out, and he was too damn tired to reach for it with his good arm and toss it out. He smiled then and rolled onto it clumsily with a half-leap and as I covered up my face as the explosion blew him to pieces. I could do nothing now but make sure the living man I had remaining in my care was kept alive as long as possible.

Suddenly I felt purpose; a man was dragging himself towards the edge of the crater. I saw his face appear as he struggled to draw himself over the lip and into safety. I moved to try and give him aid but a German sniper had other ideas. There was a single shot fired at the wounded man seeking cover and a burst of blood leaped out from the side of his head near his temple. The sods were now killing the wounded for I learnt as I dragged his body in that he had missing a leg. I shook the image from my mind and sought what I was after; his water and field dressing.

I stripped him of the essentials and then stopped dead. I looked up and there I saw a tiny bird. It had come to perch on the helmet of the man with the shattered jaw, whose helmet was blown onto the lip of the crater. I studied it for a moment and it sang to me. It was so beautiful to hear and then he flew away. Now you might call me crazy but from that moment on I knew I was to survive this day. There was something about that bird and his singing that spoke to me in clear and plain English that I was to live to see another day dawn. And as I looked at the man with the sucking chest wound I could only hope that he would also live, but I

110

wasn't about to pray for him because God didn't seem to be answering too many calls today.

I looked up into the cloudless sky; the heat was building and we were extremely thirsty. It must have been around 1430hrs when I could hear a renewed effort to take the enemy trenches from them. Whistle blasts and the sound of artillery were filling the air. The machine guns added that ghastly nightmare of a picture in my mind and after what seemed to be just minutes the scene around was quieter with the usual battle noise of machine guns, bombs, and mortars being fired; gone was the futile attack which had crumbled from existence. I was later to learn that at 1500hrs our cavalry in the rear were retired and they had been turned around and would not be joining the fighting. It may well have been that they could have saved the day for they would have been faster, breaching the points more vulnerable to attack, but no, the fighting seemed to be coming to an end.

The sun was getting lower; it was 1700hrs. Another artillery barrage had opened up. For thirty minutes they fired and I felt in my bones that generals do not learn from their mistakes. And far, far away I heard more whistle blasts as the artillery was lifted and more machine gun fire killed all of our good men. The insanity of it all is beyond description and I felt dirty.

And then it is night. The sun has gone and the sounds of battle have simmered, but there are still the machine guns of the enemy firing upon every noise they hear, trying to kill the wounded as they crawl about in an effort to get safely back to the lines. It is then that another wounded man crawls to the lip of my crater. I have my weapon ready to kill him because he might well be a sod. I call to him as I see his dark face appear and he answers with a thick Irish accent: I know it's Irish because I understand every damn word he says, and if he'd been of any other country of the BEF I would have picked it up.

This man is not too badly off. He has a wound to the leg but he'd managed to apply a field dressing of his own for when he fell he fell into a small hollow in the ground. He was lucky to be alive. He tells me that machine guns have been shooting in his direction as he moved but each time he would stop and wait a few minutes to make the gunner think that he was dead before moving again with more effort to do so quietly.

I had no water to give him but I was able to help him a little with applying a better dressing to his wound by using the fabric of the dead soldiers' uniforms. After this was done we discussed our situation and it was decided that we should try and crawl our way back as best as possible. And so it is here that I find myself crawling back towards our line with the sucking chest wound upon my back and the man with the wounded leg at my side. We do not leave each other for I can feel that these two men with me have a fear of dying alone.

We stop periodically to ensure that the sucking chest wound is still alive, and he is for most of the way back, though in extreme discomfort. When next we stop to check on him he is dead. I consider taking his pay book and ID disc for identification purposes but decide on doing the same as with the others in the crater; I leave the pay book and ID disc with him. If and when the time comes that a burial party can collect his body they will need to identify him for the grave.

There are now only two of us and we don't speak as we continue on our way. We have discarded all of our equipment but I do have my weapon. The wounded man beside me has nothing but his helmet which he fears to lose and I fear to lose the one I picked up from the crater, for although it is only a new item so recently issued it seems to be a part of me and my survival.

We continue one and have to either skirt around all the dead we come into contact with or crawl over them. It is a horrible task. There are so many dead littering the ground that the ground itself can hardly be felt. The ground is also no longer flat; the German artillery saw to that.

After what seems to be an eternity we finally get back to our trenches. There are men here who are quiet and subdued. They listen for the wounded and help get them into the trench before patching them up and getting them back to the dressing stations which are now so grossly overfilled that all the men with severe wounds are left to die in place and those that have wounds that can be managed are seen to. It is all unfair but necessary if lives are to be saved in the long term.

It is a few days later that I can reflect upon what has happened, I also learn that our division [being understrength to start with] have suffered a total of 4,692 casualties, and of all the divisions in the fighting over these past few days we have suffered the fifth highest amount. We have been decimated but once again: I hate to think what has happened to those units that have lost more.

Five days after the initial attack the medical officers have made a truce with the Germans and bodies are collected for burial. I don't waste time in seeking out the crater in which I lived for twelve hours for I didn't wish to see the faces of the dead again. I simply collected what I could and helped give them a burial. The stench of the bodies was immensely horrid and the gases built up within them sometimes escapes their orifices, but it was a task that needed to be done. Occasionally we came upon a wounded man but an extremely high number were dead.

It was then that it dawned upon me. Why hadn't Haig ensured that a proper reconnaissance had been conducted? He had air superiority; why hadn't it used it to his great advantage? Maybe he had; maybe he'd decided that regardless of the cost we had no choice but to try and break the deadlock. And so, you see, it is a war of attrition. Whoever can continue to furnish the war with fresh bodies the longest will be the winner in the end. The 2nd Royal Dublin Fusiliers is then built back up with numerous fresh men straight from home. I shall refrain from making too many friends of these but shall do all I can to ensure they learn quickly.

13th NOVEMBER 1916

It was coming on to winter once more. It wouldn't be long now and the fighting would simmer down to allow us to freeze half to death in misery. But as time wears on new aspects of war are open to us. I have heard of something new, it's called the tank. I have heard it rumbling along some place in September, and then early

113

this month had some hands on experience with it. But my story is of infantry fighting, not battles with tanks, which for all the good they did in the later stages of the war seemed not to be faring too well at all. I also saw some hand-to-hand fighting which was not something I wish to have to face again. It is one thing to kill a man from a distance whilst looking over iron sights, but something completely different to strike him down with a slash of your rifle before penetrating him with your bayonet. I have done it before now but not in the scale which has just been experienced over the past month. It is something I don't wish to think too much about. Our air superiority has also been cemented in place and does not seem to be able to be budged. I do not believe the Germans will now be able to do so well in the air for the remainder of the war.

The replacements we received after the Battle of Albert are coming along well, though they suffer the heavier casualties when stacked up against the older soldiers, but we are so few and far between that it is hard to come across an old friend.

We are at the end now of what is the Battle of the Somme, the Battle of Albert being the start and now the Battle of the Ancre [River] being the end. I'm sorry I have not reflected upon the fighting in between these two battles but you have grown in your acquaintance of war well enough to understand what it is like: even if not experienced.

We were to attack along either side of the Ancre River. With all we had learnt so far of attacking enemy in trenches, artillery support, creeping fire, machine gun positions and tanks we found ourselves in a far more comfortable position than our enemy. We were all starting to believe that we could win the war but it wouldn't be done at a stroke nor so easily awarded, but it was achievable and in sight.

Although not all objectives were taken during the battle, II Corps were rewarded with being able to take and hold all of theirs. Haig was extremely happy and content with what we had achieved but it seemed that Gough wanted more. But Gough's efforts to take more than he could chew found little solace in anything more and all he was rewarded with were excessive casualties. Of the many objectives marked on Gough's map he only managed to take and hold ground at a place called Desire Trench. It all seemed futile to me however for on the 18th we all settled down for the winter and there were no more attacks to be seen until the winter was over with.

I guess that the most important thing for me during November was that on the 16th day of this month we moved from the 10th Division to… to the 48th Brigade, 16th Division [the 16th Irish Division]. Oh, yes. We again had suffered heavy casualties but now reinstated and with men of our own background. I felt as though this was a great award being bestowed upon me. Don't get me wrong, please; I love the English, but I love the Irish even more.

INTERMISSION

Yes; intermission; what a word, but that's exactly how Christmas felt to me, an intermission between phases of war. War for months without break and then time to freeze to death; and so, Happy New Year; you bastards. I look forward to shooting you sods down into this bloody mud and stinking filth, and hope the lice are eating you as much as they are eating me. Take a running jump back to where you belong.

And it would appear that they heard me for in February they withdraw, all through March until April, to what they called the Hindenburg Line. The proof was in the pudding as I've heard spoken on many occasions and the Germans have suffered so badly in this war that they have no decent men left to fight it. They are so thin on the ground that they have to withdraw to a smaller frontage, one which has been fortified using the forced labour of prisoners, both civil and of war. The Hindenburg Line, a defence system like none we have come across before, a new front line some thirty miles shorter than what we had been used to. But not only did this free up thirteen enemy divisions to act as reserve but it also allowed us to reinforce ours. Did this mean that attacks in the future would constitute more waves and hence more dead and dying? Only time would tell.

What was this new line made of; why, concrete bunkers and gun emplacements, dug outs and command posts which put all others to shame; exceptional trenches and tunnels connected the lot. We thought we'd seen everything until we saw the line. The sod is to be congratulated, but then again it was by the forced labour of POWs that this grand structure of defence was possible, but not our POWs, or so I have been informed, but those of Russia. Maybe there is propaganda here, too; the sod advising the Russians that we are a common enemy. And so we find ourselves on the doorstep of the Arras Offensive and the officers in charge seem to be weathering poorly under the pressures of the war.

Winter is over with and a new year of war begun, but the tell-tale signs of distress can be seen everywhere, in particular with the officers. Those officers who had served longer than others seemed to be more affected with complaints of poor health: headaches, heart rates, involuntary shaking of the hands. Was it because they felt partly responsible for sending men to their death on a daily basis? One in every forty men were officers, yet one in every seventeen were of officer rank, so their life expectancy was a lot less than ours: but I cannot for the life of me consider men like Haig as an officer of men. Officers like Haig don't see war as we do; they simply send us 'to-it' before wiping their hands and reaching for a cup of nice hot tea whilst we attend our lice and other misgivings in life as its exists on the front.

9th APRIL 1917

We are at the Battle of Arras and what a week it has been. There has been a preliminary bombardment of Vimy Ridge as of the 20th March and this was extended to the remainder of the sector on the 4th April prior to our departure over the lines of no return. It is a wonder they call it that. Is it to mean that we shall not return to it alive, or that the attack will be so easily won, just like the Battle of Albert, and a walk-over is expected, in which case there will be no going back? I'm sick to death of the assurances given by the officers sitting in there dugouts and bunkers of luxury when compared to the miserable conditions under which we live, but it is their task I suppose to try with all their effort to keep up morale. Maybe they should stop the MPs from killing deserters and cowards; this would relieve tensions, and probably increase the number of deserters, but shouldn't a proper court of law decide the fate of men so struck with the fear of death? Hard labour and perpetual imprisonment would be a far better tact, but I doubt for a second it's easy for someone whose gone insane to think clearly about their actions before they conduct them. Besides, it is not my position to truly decide the fate of a coward, which is why others get paid a fortune to make these decisions and I get paid a shilling a day to live in shit up to my armpits. What about those blasted cowards at home who refuse to come to war?

Already the smell of cordite is in the air and so strong that it makes some men physically sick, but it helps hide the smell of death, and the lights of the night sky, flares here and there, give an alternate satisfaction even if for just a few moments of solace during quiet nights.

There has been another commotion sprung to life. Just three days ago America declared war upon Germany. It came about almost two whole years after the sinking of the RMS Lusitania by a sodding U-boat. It still amazes me today how long it took the Americans to join the fight and as I lived well into my 70s I was also bemused by the Americans late entry into the Second World War. But who am I to judge their reasoning; I'm just happy that they went as far as to provide materials for us to meet the war head-on, for without that aid we may well have lost everything, including my lovely wife and our children, one of which I have never met and the other I've seen but once. Further news is herald in regards to the Americans joining the war; it will be more than a year before they are ready to fight. Yes indeed; they will come and join us when the war is almost over and take the accolades for a job well done. They come with the conscripts from England but are obviously more ambitious.

Mining and tunnelling prior to the Battle of Arras was extremely excessive, so excessive it would seem that not all of the tunnels built purposely for detonating were left intact for the simple reason that the generals didn't wish to impede the infantry during the opening phases of battle due to the ground being churned up too much, but to get an insight into the actual depth in which mining and tunnelling was conducted I must give you some examples: it's simply mind-boggling, pure and simple.

Facts and figures can me moved around far too much but I shall give them how I understand them. Just in one of the sectors around Arras there were four tunnelling companies who made up a force of 2,000 men in total; these worked around the clock, twenty-four hours a day in eighteen hour shifts for two months. All of this was to aid us in getting men and supplies to the front in the safest environment possible. The tunnels were actually an addition to what already existed for the ground of Arras was chalky and good for digging, there also was to be found many caverns, underground quarries and sewage tunnels; to this was added over 12 miles of what is deemed as 'subways', 'tramways' and' railways' ['foot traffic', 'hand-drawn trolleys' and 'light railway']. It all came with underground electricity, latrines, kitchens, casualty facility and able to hide 24,000 men. And who was responsible for digging it all; Mostly New Zealanders and Bantams [men under the regulation height of 5 foot 3 inches]. 200 men were either killed or wounded through the sods efforts to counter-mine ours, and although 10 per cent is high it could have been a hell of a lot worse.

But enough talk on this for it is zero hour and a Monday, Easter Sunday having just gone. It's 0530hrs and the earth has been moved with a horrendous bombardment of five minutes' worth of body-and-bunker shattering artillery fire; another five minutes of shelling; further shells to add to that already fired; over 2,689,000 in total.

118

MY GOD! This is ludicrous! What lengths are we going to in order to kill each other; its sheer madness!

And that's not all. We added gas shells for the fun of it. The ground on the enemy side of the fence no longer looked like a well-constructed trench but a land of craters with pockets of Germans still prepared to defend the land they sit upon. They also fought well in the air during this period, despite the fact that we had air superiority. On the scene was the Red Baron but I'll refrain from speaking on the matter for too much on the subject of Manfred von Richtholfen and his infamous squadron will draw your attention away from my story.

I was moments from propelling myself into the air in order to be on my way when a huge fragment of artillery, which exploded not very far away, shot past me and embedded itself inches from my gut and covering me in dirt. I thank my lucky star that I was still alive and then saw something hanging there. It was an ancient axe head from centuries past, a relic of the Roman Empire long gone. I wasted not a second and grabbed it up, thrust it away inside my khakis, and was on my way into battle.

Over the next few weeks I took part in two major battles; both the first and second Scarpe. The battles of the offensive are as follows:

First Battle of the Scarpe, 9th – 14th April;
Battle of Vimy Ridge, 9th – 12th April;
First Battle of Bullecourt, 11th April;
Battle of Lagnicourt, 15th April;
Second Battle of the Scarpe, 23rd – 24th April;
Battle of Arleux, 28th – 29th April
Third Battle of the Scarpe, 3rd – 4th April;
Second Battle of Bullecourt, 3rd – 17th May;

The offensive officially ended on the 16th day of May and was considered a British victory but I fail to see how a victory can be scored when you suffer more casualties than the opposition. It is fair to say we managed our objectives well but there was no exploitation to be granted us. There was little to be gained strategically and the French offensive at the Aisne did not go at all well: again with the damn French and their inabilities. All in all we suffered 158,660 casualties and the sod received anything up to 130,000; so there lays the truth and the truth is that this was a war of attrition and had little to do with gaining ground and tackling exploitation of objectives in a manner safe enough to save our souls from perpetual hell.

Gains made during the offensive were good to quite good with the best gains made in the centre of the line and the less favourable being towards the south at Bullecourt but the offensive soon reverted back to a stalemate of trench facing trench and spending time with the rats and the lice.

May I now tell you this? The offensive since past was a holiday compared to what was to come and I'm sure most of you already know what it is that I speak of.

30th MAY 1917

What are my forethoughts?

Firstly; that there have been so many tunnels dug beneath our feet these past three years that any water upon the surface should surely drain away. Secondly; that I wouldn't wish this experience upon my worst enemy but glad that I suffered it so that my children and children's children won't have to.

I am so naïve.

Once again the softening up of the enemy has commenced. The preliminary bombardment had commenced in some areas on the 21st but others just today. It is a tell-tale sign that something it about to happen; a free signal to the enemy to watch his front; but the enemy might consider it a ruse, but how the hell can you honestly explain the use of so many artillery shells upon an objective which you have no intention of attacking, in particular when resources are so low. And where is this bombardment I speak of taking place, but of course, this is the prelude to the slaughter of Passchendaele, that horrible place which sits in my memory forever and upon the summit of the slopes which draws the salient that is Ypres into its menacing jaws. The prelude I speak of is nothing to what was to occur but a stepping stone is just that and needs to be explained, even if minutely.

It boggles the mind to see the dirt fly into the air during any bombardment around Ypres for if you are nearer the town on a clear day and look towards England you can see and feel a quiet reminiscence of what is the English Channel in sight. You turn again to look east and see the earth being torn apart, the ground which will turn to mud, for although there has been extremely little rain these past weeks the weather was to soon make up for it and as we all know, a little rain adds something disastrous to stirred-up dirt, turning it into one gigantic and foul bog. Yes; that is Flanders for you. Again it seems here that God is against us all. So little rain and what water the farmers have in their wells they lock up tight with padlocks so that the soldiers have to revert to vandalism; we have to break the locks to steal the water because there is none to be had. Let's hope that none of us gets caught for it wouldn't go down well to be shot simply because we were thirsty and that the resupply system was not working well in our favour.

The Battle of Messines I took no part but further up the line the 16th Irish, of which you'll recall I was now a member, were assigned Wytschaete [in reality we were further to the south on the line of attack]. These are two villages and the distance between – around nine miles – was symbolic of any strategic objective and constituted a ridge of some importance. I shall speak only briefly upon these attacks for they allowed us to position ourselves for the hell I have referred to which was the Third Battle of Ypres, or Passchendaele; so let's get on with the story for the memory of it all is burning inside my head and I wish to be rid of the pain it causes.

The sod is retaliating and returning fire but his 630 guns is no match for the 2,266 artillery pieces and 757 heavy guns of ours that continue with their initial task and complement this with counter-battery fire: over 3,000,000 shells before the whistle on the 7th. The science of war is sometimes marvellous but the manner of attrition in the lines soon draws your attention away from such progress. It's as though everything that has occurred to me during this horrid war has surpassed everything else I had done before it and after. Having lived through it all and approaching old age I can look back upon it and know it is the reason that life has been little more than an anti-climax. Nothing can compare to the suffering and the suffering in turn lingers for a lifetime, draining our souls of all happiness to such a degree that nothing we do can really cheer us up to such heights that war can be forgotten. Yes, looking upon your children and grandchildren do bring a smile upon your face but you are soon reminded by that devil in your head that they smile because of the sacrifices of other men, sacrifices that we are all grateful for: huh; 'all of us are grateful for' indeed; all of us except those bastards in government who made false promises to those that served in the trenches, to come home and find their jobs gone and the cowards rich through the expenses of human flesh and decay.

7th JUNE 1917

I had learnt, being sometime after the war, that the initial idea of the attacks in which we carried out over the next few months were done so in order to carry out a victory in the seizure of key areas; these areas could be more simply defined as the German U-boat pens which had access to the North Sea and from there caused all manner of war fatality, even civilian as you have learnt, without so much as a shudder of guilt or recognition, the U-boats scouring the Atlantic for easy targets and targets of opportunity, which mean the same to me, and deliver their payloads expectantly in defence against those that stood in their way, in particular vessels of the British Merchant Navy transporting ammunition for the war effort and food for those poor wretches at home half starving to death.

The hope was to do this with some measure of secrecy and surprise but how much surprise can you obtain when the sod can see you moving copious amounts of men and arms into an area which is being raked bare by vicious artillery fire for days on end? If the Germans were bright then they would lie back a little and build their reserve for what was to come and whether or not this was done to any worthwhile degree is doubtful for we did manage to gain some ground during the time of Passchendaele.

Once more the operation relied on its old friend the mine, and in this case we had 21 in total all ready to be exploded beneath the sodding soil of the sods' trenches. It is a wonder that such extensive mining was never discovered but there is always a way in which to deceive the enemy, such as digging a mine long enough towards the enemy and then setting up a hammer upon a pulley which could be operated some distance away, manipulated in such a way that it banged upon a sheet of metal or wood and drawing the sods' ears away from our prized possessions. Our teams of miners also had an instrument called a geophone. It was similar to a stethoscope but consisted of a round ball being pushed into the clay surface of the mine wall and connected to this was a tube then fed into both ears. We could now be sure as to whether or not counter-mining had been implemented by the sod upon our hoax and determine whether or not our other mines remained reasonably safe.

At 0310hrs on this day 19 of the 21 mines were detonated, 1,000,000 pounds of explosive set in motion, a huge portion of the German line and support network utterly obliterated, 10,000 German dead at the drop of a hat, the explosion so loud it was easily heard in London. Can you image that; what it would have been like? Can you image further more being a mother at home in London being woken by the noise of the explosion and the tears welling in her eyes for the fear of what must have caused such a horrendous blast?

Parts of Hill 60 was still in the sky when the whistle blew but these finer particles of dirt was nothing compared to the initial scene when the entire surface of the world appeared in the air, large chunks of rock and earth along with the bodies of men as high as could possibly be seen. It was filled with flame and debris, and enemy bunkers made of reinforced concrete were bowled over as though made of paper. The shaking and rumbling of the earth even affected our own trenches but to an obvious lesser degree.

The crescendo of the barrage had not abated but commenced to creep towards the enemy with our good men following behind it. The wounded we suffered from our own demise were fewer than what would have been suffered if the sod was shooting at us with interlocking machine guns or artillery of his own so we cared little for the small sacrifice of a few, for so many had been saved. This in fact was the first time that the attacking force fatalities were lighter than those of the defending team. We had turned around the usual result of war and as an attacking force were coming out on top; but how long would it last?

The taking of Messines Ridge was an important stride towards securing Wytschaete and then the sites further afield, but the pens which housed the U-boats were not to be taken, for Haig on the 23rd September would be forced to cancel his decision due to our progress across Flanders.

By 0500hrs Messines was ours; by 0900hrs we had taken Wytschaete. It was such a smashing victory that we were instilled with great waves of relief and proud stability; but again, how long would it last?

This was a time to celebrate but no time was given. Our tanks were here and worked… as well as can be expected, and the sodding retaliation of counterattack was repulsed so easily; it was as though a dream was coming true. Could the end of the war truly be in sight?

Can we give praise to the tanks for this momentous success or is it all explosions and guts that provide the reward of victory? Do you know how tanks came to be? Originally cast to be a team of two men this was the dream of Churchill. The two men were to act so; one man would ride a motorcycle and the other would fire the mounted machinegun upon it from his sidecar, but trench warfare saw that the idea had far too many restraints and that its long leash of operational abilities was stunted by the conditions and scenarios. And what use is it to have highly trained men and nothing to make of them, and so Churchill devised the idea of ships to sail upon the land, huge tubs to plaster the enemy with hot lead, and they looked like water tanks. The Motor Machine Section of the Machine Gun Corps was now operating out of tanks.

In fewer than twelve hours of fighting, not only were Messines and Wytschaete ours but other objectives were in hand as well with more than 7,000 enemy prisoners taken. There is one further thing to tell you which I think is rather important, in particular considering the fighting in Ireland which I spoke of earlier, and that was that we, the 16th Irish, and for the first time ever, were fighting side-by-side with the 36th Ulsters… North and South… Protestant and Catholic… and a mix of atheist here and there but love for country more than making up for it all. A man cannot always choose the company he keeps. Sometimes a man might be born a Protestant but have the heart of a Catholic. Some things remain secret, but the bond that men have as brothers exceeds all else.

And so the night is falling upon us and the rubble of Wytschaete is not far when the first of many grand memories recite their masked beauty, usually unheard for the noise of war is so loud but on this occasion something to be held dear to heart. It was fairly warm for there was no rain and the night had brought out the nightingales. Their singing was a comfort seldom found in war. It was bliss. None of us cares about what the other believes, we only care that they live and breathe, and that we help each other in this time of great need.

We were victorious and the dry weather was killing us through heat and poor water replenishment, and the phase of the operation calling for the capture of the U-boat pens seemed but so close. And so we waited and the generals talked. For two months there was little to nothing occurring worth me telling you about other than a new time table of bombardment commencing on the 16th day of July. With the passing of time the sod improved his fortifications; with the passing of time went the summer months and approaching was a month or more of heavy rain.

It was coming up to the Third Battle of Ypres and the sods had invented another gas to be used against the flesh and bone of our good men and cause. It had various names but the one that sticks in my mind is 'GAS!' for all apparent reasons. Call it HS [Hun Stuff] if you like, it doesn't matter much, but the word that gets in your ear when most needed to hear is the clear and concise calling of gas. The sods called it Yellow Cross because on their artillery firing line they had stacks of gas shells and needed to differentiate between one and the other, so, chlorine gas was marked with a green cross and the mustard gas with a yellow one.

It was soon learnt that mustard gas was far more effective at killing, maiming, and clearing the trenches as chlorine gas, and it certainly did like to linger. Delivered in artillery shells it polluted the ground upon which we lived, soaking into the soil and remaining for anything up to a month or more, which was highly dependent on the atmospheric conditions of the time. It was heavier than air and so didn't act by similar contrast to its cousin the chlorine, but it could easily be reactivated by a little digging or shelling. One always had to be on their toes and know the history of the ground on which they were on for the more one knew of his surrounds the better the precautions could be taken.

Having said all of this the dangers were sometimes ignored, for although it was a deadly weapon and accounted for 90% of all deaths caused by gas, if a man had to dig then he had to dig and after several years in the field one trench looked much like the other: although some of the trenches dug by the French were extremely inadequate and I assume it is because of their philosophy of wanting to be on the attack and to keep the momentum moving other than sitting in place and waiting to be attacked: but then again there were so many instances where this could be proved incorrect. It was all well and good, but the French failed to deliver on this philosophy when needed for the counterattacks at the Second Battle of Ypres and others.

The effects of mustard gas was blistered skin and sore eyes, vomit accompanied with internal bleeding. It was painful at best and excruciating at worse and some of the men who inhaled it sufficiently enough could take up to five weeks to die from the exposure. Worst of all you did not need to breathe it in to feel the effects of it; simply contact with the skin was enough to cause blistering. Many a time did I see the flesh of men being eaten away by high concentrations of mustard gas where contact with the skin started what would become an evacuation process, red sores turning into blister accompanied by headaches, fluid on the lung and high temperature.

This was a double-edged weapon if ever there was. Any general worth his salt and pepper, as I sometimes like to say, wouldn't allow the use of mustard gas prior to an attack by his troops where ground was the main prize over casualties, for the lingering effect of the gas meant it dealt just as much suffering to the axis as the allies. But as experienced in the past the generals of the sods seemed to care little for the conscripts which were forced to party under the banner of the Kaiser, that damn sod, the biggest of them all, that looked at himself in the mirror each day and saw a glorious German emperor instead of a ghastly monster. What did he care of the innocent, those young men fighting for rights of freedom due every man and woman?

Those poor men that drew large wafts of gas into their lungs obviously suffered the most where other were more fortunate and only suffered a little, but the effects of the gas remained with us for the remainder of our lives in most cases. Respiratory disease was one thing to deal with in old age; failing eyesight another. You might image how men felt being returned to the front, to continue with the fight after being given the all clear by medical practitioners, knowing that their lungs were not quite right for scar tissue had formed and would be a permanent reminder of the sodden German attacks of immoral purity, for tuberculosis was common.

It is unlike any other wound for it cannot be bandaged. And the burns are agonizing, far worse than any other wound I fear. You can't help but cry out for the endurance of pain is far more outlasting than a man's conviction to accept it.

Different gas had different affects but all can easily be condemned, in particular by the nurses who treated the poor wounded. The chlorine gas burned heavily in the throat and eyes with that suffocation feeling. Sever pains in the centre of the chest, coughing, retching, trouble breathing which was often rapid though shallow, vomiting, dryness of the throat, headaches and imbalance when stood up.

There is acute bronchitis or bronchopneumonia develops; the temperature rises to as high as 104. Delusion sets in, Pleurisy may occur, and gangrene of the lung might follow.

But recovery is sometimes attained after which the patient remains exhausted and unable to perform any duties for quite some time. The nervous system is affected and headaches, vertigo and dyspepsia may continue for several weeks.

Those that recovered sufficiently to be redeployed into the trenches were due to their exposure being classed as mild but only after the lungs had proved to be clear of the affects any gas. Others suffer permanent incapacity and may experience Blighty leave, though little joy there can be in just a joyous occasion for it would be far better to return with a leg missing than being incapacitated by gas.

And what about the evacuation plan; what can be said about it? It was as good as could be expected under the circumstance, except for at the Somme.

Many stages existed, but some men might miss one or more stages due to their injury. And not all men with injuries could be attended to for those that were seen to be dying were left aside whilst others that could be saved were treated.

The first port of call was our Regimental Aid Post normally situated just behind the front and in the reserve trenches. Have a bandage applied, grab a drink, be sent off further down the line as soon as practically possible. This is what you might term as 'light first aid'. Although the officer was a medical officer the others would be less endowed and from the ranks of the infantry itself:

though each and every one would be accustomed to dressing wounds and diagnosing sufficiently enough to remedy minor treatment.

Then on to the Advanced Dressing Station 'ADS'. Different means were employed to get men along and if they could walk then they did so under their own presence. There was also a good system of Stretcher Bearer relay established after the first two years of war whereby men were stationed at 1000 yards apart. This didn't only aid in fewer cases of exhaustion through portage of men but also allowed familiarity with the changing landscape of their particular sector.

Further along and there was the Main Dressing Station.

Regimental details were again a formality before the next stop along the line to the rear, again depending on the severity of the wound/s, which was the Field Ambulance. More time was available for treatment here but again the urgency for quick evacuation was always present. Emergency operations were able to be carried out at the Field Ambulance but only where really necessary or time permitted. A Field Ambulance had capacity for around 150 casualties but were often inundated which saw many men lying around upon stretchers awaiting further development or death. Limb amputations would be done at the CCS.

The CCS, or Casualty Clearing Station, was next in line, wounded moved on by any reasonable means such as horse and carriage, ambulance train, canal barge, or other wagon transport. These were usually well equipped facilities set up in a tented camp. From here you would either be treated and returned to the front, remain in place for specialist surgery in readiness for further movement down the line, or keep the wheels turning by sending on the worst but stable cases to other more suited facilities. The CCS could hold 1,000 wounded.

The Base Hospitals were next in the line of evacuation or possibly even good old England for those that had been granted the identity of 'Blighty'.

A Base Hospital would provide a great opportunity for life and holding over 1,000 patients to 2,500 and provided ample facility for most if not all injuries sustained on the front. Places on the coast such as Boulogne and Le Havre had base hospitals as well as Le Touquet, Rouen and Etaples. But enough of this; to battle we go.

I am not a weatherman but I know that an airstream is approaching towards us and we can feel it in our bones. There is much rain upon the wind of this airstream and we shall feel the full brunt of its unseen power to come.

31st JULY 1917

The Third Battle of Ypres is said to be between the 31st July and 10th November. The period was more or less the same with the exemption that engineering progress was made in regards to walkways [duckboards] allowing for slightly easier movement from the front to the rear and vice versa. The objective was the village of Passchendaele and the securing of the coast. As well as the usual infantry and artillery there was to be 168 Mark IV tanks [48 in reserve] with five divisions of cavalry to be deployed.

The initial wonderment was as grand as the last Allied effort, with creeping barrage and infantry assault with tanks securing a 4,000 yards breakthrough, but German counterattacks took back most of this from our exhausted troops. What happened next was unprecedented for in August the weather turned extremely foul. 25mm of rain was suffered for three days from the 1st August to 4th August; a further 10mm was now added to that which could not escape the mud stricken ground on the 8th. On the night of the 11th the sky broke out in horrendous, blistering rain and lightning for a further three days.

Regardless of the weather, however, the Battle of Langemarck must be fought, and at the forefront of it all I find myself once more in a bad place.

16th AUGUST 1917

We were extremely exhausted and many of the men suffered from some form of illness but stuck it out as best they could. My brigade was at the front, and the 2nd Dublin was just behind the two leading units: the 7th Royal Irish Rifles and the 9th Dublin Fusiliers to our front. I guess I can consider myself extremely lucky but fail to see much luck in the conditions we are made to attack over. There is little semblance of anything at all to our front, such a massive marchland void of any trees, shrubs or grass and behind us were the duckboards that had delivered us this far. It is mud and mud alone which is covered in craters all filled with water. The water has nowhere to go and so these holes in the ground swallow men whole. It's hard to keep on ones feet when the going is rough and you're being shot at. You have to take cover; have to run; and needless to say you slip and fall down time-and-time again. If you should fall into a crater then you can count your blessings having been paid in full if you should live for so many die through the sheer exhaustion of holding on to dear life or being drowned in the muck straight away.

We commenced the attack at 0445hrs and so it is rather dark; it is hard to see where you are and where you are going. You can only hope that you aren't heading for the deepest crater there is, for if you are there will be no returning. But before we have even left the line to commence our assault we have lost 65 per cent of our men to the sodding artillery. Can you imagine that, going into battle when two-thirds of you are either dead or dying even before the whistle?

German machineguns then open up and we are decimated once again. How many times must it be like this? So many times my unit is decimated and I come that much closer to dying. But I again must thank my lucky stars for B Coy have but five soldiers left alive whilst I, under charge of C Coy, move in to give aid to a stricken 9th Dublin Fusiliers who have lost every single solitary man in their battalion except two officers and ten other ranks. Can you see now, dear reader, what it is to be 'decimated'?

And so we continue on with the pain of knowing we are so few and suddenly I find myself up to my armpits in mud. Men are passing me by for it is hard to see and there is a war going on but I yell as loudly as I possibly can but it is useless because no one will hear me, and so I try to wave my arms about and slip to my chin in mud. A man then stumbles and I have no idea who it is. I think he is dead but he isn't. He has seen my plea for aid and soon there are three men taking the time to get me out of there against their orders and whilst being blindly sprayed by enemy machineguns trying to find their marks with the aid of flares. They use their rifles and with great effort I grasp to of these with my muddy paws and am fortunate enough to be dragged out of my predicament. My saviours then re-join the attack and instantly two of them are killed but the other continues on. I follow immediately after with the weight of the stinking mud slowing me down.

The sun is trying to come up above the horizon. As it comes I can see the landscape more clearly. I can see the miserable scene about where bodies decay all around me and there are limbs of men lying here and there: an arm and a leg, then more on top of that; oh, and a head torn from the body with its eyes looking up into the sky searching for the gates into heaven. There are scores of smashed up wagons, tanks, and other articles of war. I can see horses so thin that their skin seems sucked into their bodies with the ribs scoring into the hide, almost worn away from the effects of death and the bad weather. Spouts of mud and water shoot into the air where artillery shells land and machineguns find their targets by using the spouts of water shooting up from craters as points of reference in order to secure a kill. The bodies have been laying around here for anything up to two whole weeks or more and cannot be moved. It is a wasted effort to drag in the dead when so much energy is taken to drag in the wounded, and even then the wounded are lucky to be given aid at all.

This was the mud of Passchendaele and we all knew that the attacks would not be called off.

If I was careful I might survive and then a machinegun burst whizzed past my head. I struck the ground hard but the fall was cushioned by the mud and I was half buried in it as I lay flat upon my stomach in an effort to clear myself from view of the enemy gunner. I crawled further forward and made an effort to get up with the weight of the mud clinging to my body and the machinegun burst upon me again but this time I stayed down and crawled further forward in the hope of getting past the bunkers visual. I came upon a crater lip and was astonished by what I saw.

Below me in a crater about ten feet across were two wounded men and another dead. It was the Somme all over again. Just before plunging in I lifted my head to see what lay before me and what I saw was the bunker once more and further afield yet another. I pulled my head down and slid into the crater where the two living saw me but remained silent through their misery and helplessness.

I could hear the sounds of war continuing on all around me but was hard pressed to ever see anything; everyone was so covered in mud that they blended in with the surrounds and the only hope of seeing anyone was if they moved. I then reflected upon the bunkers and realised how hard it was to actually see them for they too were camouflaged in the mud slung up from artillery fire. There must have been scores of men in small pockets of resistance putting fire down upon the sod as the sod was putting fire down upon us. It was a stalemate once more and no man was going anywhere, and fast. If nothing else this must have been a great scenario for all those snipers wishing to increase their number of kills.

It was then that one of the wounded men made acquaintance by referring to how hard it was to see the bunker not far to our front and so I chanced another look, and knew I must be pressing my luck, and indeed managed to make out a bunker looking directly down upon us. It must have been them that had been firing at me and then I realised that the bunkers would have been shooting across the front of the bunkers either side of it and not directly to its front, hence a criss-cross effect of fire being formed, an enfilade fire in direct support of the other bunkers which formed an impenetrable wall of fire that could not be crossed by flesh and blood. The only time in fact that the bunkers switched their firing to their front was when in danger of being overrun or bombed by my specialised infantry counterparts. I was easy to see therefore that there was no going forward and no going back. To go forward would be into the face of a machinegun and its crew; to go back would be through the impenetrable wall of fire... to stay put was simply crazy.

I took to evaluating the wounded and found that both had similar wounds. Both were riddled with bullet holes in their left and right arms, a miraculous coincidence. Both were in sheer agony whenever they moved their limbs and therefore found it difficult to check their wounds and treat them effectively, and so with the mud wallowing up to my waste as I crouched in the centre of the crater I drew myself closer to the side and tried with all my effort to get my feet planted into the mud substantially enough to keep me steady.

I asked if the two wounded were managing okay in preventing themselves from slipping further into the mud and they answered yes, for they were leaning upon the side of the crater with their feet firmly upon the backs of their dead comrades: two dead men below the surface of the mud were allowing these two wounded to remain adrift as it were.

There was no way to clean the wounds and so all I could do was try to fasten them more securely, which I managed to do within ten minutes.

A Lewis-gun was then heard and it sounded quite close; not more than 100 feet away. The enemy retaliate and the Lewis-gun fell silent. I never heard from them again. They could have withdrawn; maybe they were playing dead; or maybe they were killed or wounded. But I had to consider my position as best I could.

I looked at the dead man once my task was complete and felt myself slip into the mud. I knew I had to stay still or drown, but what was to happen if I fell asleep in my exhaustion and drowned?

The two wounded were certainly in no way able to give me aid. Another 30 minutes must have passed when one of the wounded said the one thing that was already on my mind. I would have to take the dead man and use his body to keep me afloat. This was the one thing I didn't want to do but did I have a choice in the matter. During the Somme I refrained from taking a wounded man's pay book but this time I reached out and searched his body. I took his pay book and ID discs and then found something more. I found a letter from his wife or girlfriend, for there was also a photo alongside it. I wasn't game to read it: I would leave that to the officers in the rear when they returned his belongings to England. I also found a fob watch which was not working. It seemed to have a dent in it which was put there by a bullet. Maybe it saved his life once and so he maintained it as a good luck charm, as some men do with these things.

I was about to remove his equipment from his body but one of the wounded men said no, it would be better to stand upon him fully dressed. So this soldier was now an 'it'. So I took it and managed to push it before me and then down under my feet. I now had something good to stand on but my conscience would play hell with me in future years.

Some time later, I don't know how long exactly, I fell asleep. I woke again just before dark when a light rain began to fall. It was very light but still added to our misery. We were caked in mud, unable to move, freezing cold, without much more than half a canteen of water between three men and some iron rations which would parch me further.

What were we to do?

I went into a bit of a trance at that moment. I knew that there were places upon the line which were being relieved now and again, as was the routine in the trenches. After eight days I could possibly count on being relieved. I could only assume that this would be all the sooner due to the poor conditions and the inability to get stores up to the men holding the line, and then I did an amazing thing; I smiled. One of the wounded looked at me as though I was mad and I thought again about our position. Here we were, thin on the ground with pockets of resistance scattered around; some places on the line faring better than ours. We were at what appeared a stalemate. The Germans obviously saw no great need to attack us, unless it was a counter-attack to take back valuable ground lost; but that wasn't the case for me, surely. I tried with my entire might to listen for Lewis-guns and Lee-Enfields firing, and the darker it became the easier it was to distinguish, but there was always the retaliation of returned fire from the sod to deal with.

No; it was hopeless. To stay here was a death sentence. I had to try and get the two wounded men back but should I take the worst case or the better. I looked at the two wounded and they looked at me. I explained what I intended to do, to try and get back to our line with both of them, but obviously could only manage one at a time. They decided for me. Leave the worst case behind for his pain was not as great, but his wounds extremely bad. I accepted this decision and loosened my haversack, pulling my arms free from it as it was stuck in the mud. If nothing else it had helped keep my back warm.

With the sun now down and my chances of getting the wounded back all the more sure I made my way as best I could to a position behind the wounded man before trying to pull him up and out, this was brought to a quick close as some flares appeared just above us. I fell to the ground and waited, a mouthful of mud for my trouble. The next opportunity was farer but the wounded man wouldn't budge. He was stuck hard in the mud when I suddenly realised he hadn't undone his haversack. With this now undone I tried again to lift him out; again he wounded move. His feet and waist were so well stuck in the mud that it was going to take all of my strength and analysis to achieve my aim.

I soon noticed without too much effort that my feet, even outside of the crater, had sunk into the mud up to my knees as I pulled and pulled, but there was still no movement from the wounded and his body from the waist down just would not give an inch. It was then decided against our wishes to try the other soldier but again, no matter how hard we tried he simply wouldn't move. I clambered back into the hole before another flare chanced into the sky above me and chewed upon the dilemma that faced us.

There was no doubt at all that I was unable to move either man and to do this I would need serious aid. I was therefore confronted with two options. Firstly, to stay put and wait for relief, watching over my two companions [but we were out of water and dressings]; secondly, I could go back myself and get a stretcher party to follow me back out to this crater. Neither option sounded great but little choice there was to choose from. If we stayed we would probably die and so back to the line I would have to go.

I commenced to make my way to the far side of the crater and heard whispering in the cold night air between the cracks of rifle fire and artillery; this I ignored and climbed the side with great effort. Once at the lip I heard further whispering. I stopped and turned around covered in mud and looked into the eyes of the wounded as best I could in the light made available by the motions of war. I could just make out the whites of their eyes and see their hands moving around before them as shadows danced around. They knew as well as I that the chances of survival were slim. Wasn't it bad enough that I should have to go back to our own line, let alone come back out to the crater? We all knew from experience that the task was enormous. Their wounds were bad and they'd lost a lot of blood. They would also require two stretcher parties of 6 to 8 men a-piece. The war was lost for them and we all knew it. I then saw a grenade appear in one of the men's hands I thought for a dying moment that they meant to commit suicide, but all I could hear was a simple statement advising me that the grenade was for the enemy if they should chance too close.

I turned and commenced my journey.

I shall not tell you the story of my return to our own lines for the trek was a long one. I should guess that I set out from the crater at around 2000hrs and by the time I'd gotten back to our own line and support it was well past midnight. The reason it took so long is because many of the duckboards that we'd employed the day before to get to the front were actually missing; having either sunk or been hit directly by artillery; and once your path is lost it is lost, it was also unfortunate and hard to admit that on my way back I only managed to fall upon a duckboard because I was approaching it from an acute angle: in other words, I was going in the wrong direction and instead of towards my lines I was crossing in front of them. There was absolutely no way in which I was going to manage with a wounded man on my back, and then in dawned upon me. How in the hell was I going to find them again?

I could tell you how we made an effort to get to the men but this wasn't until the following night, and we failed miserably to find those we were looking for but managed to get seven wounded men back who were a little closer to the line than they were. The amount of wounded men out there amongst the mud was atrocious. When I was returning on my own from the pit of despair, in which I had found myself emotionally and physically, I simply couldn't fathom the numbers of bodies I saw laying around. At one stage I heard gurgling noises and wondered aimlessly for a dozen feet to see what I could find, but all there was, was an empty hole from what I could manage to see. Maybe it was another man drowning in the mud, or the gasses of his body escaping the tomb in which it was set: for the stench about was putrid to say the least. And later still I reflected upon this short journey of mine which seemed to last forever and that it never occurred to me that many of the bodies I saw may have been wounded, but either unconscious or sleeping. But what can a single man do against such overwhelming odds.

And so I never again laid eyes upon the two men that I shared a crater with again, but in the least I returned the letter with the photo of the young woman; her husband – and I wish to think of him as that – had saved my life.

By the 22nd August, some 23 days since the commencement of the Third Battle of Ypres, we had suffered 3,420 officer casualties and 64,586 other ranks; many of whom were missing in the mud and would never be found again. May they all rest in peace.

And so time continues ever on. The Battle of Menin Road was undertaken from 20th to 25th September, 3,500,000 rounds of artillery fired in predatory, almost four times more than that of 31st July; we gained 1.5 miles in ground.

The Battle of Polygon Wood on 26th September saw another gain of more than one mile, and on the 4th October the Battle of Broodseinde saw the Australiana deliver a smashing victory where their heroics shall never be forgotten.

The 9th October saw the Battle of Poelcappelle come and go and the First Battle of Passchendaele arrived in earnest on 12th October.

The Second Battle of Passchendaele commenced on the 26th and ended on the 10th November.

But what is the meaning of all these dates and battles?

4th October – clouds filled the sky and it rained, adding more to that which had fell this past two weeks… 6th October – the bad weather showed not a single sign of slowing up… 11th October – hurricane force winds on the eve of battle… 13th October – it rained non-stop for fifteen solid hours….

Was it not always the same, that rain preceded an attack, which shortly after there might be a little sunshine to dry up the rain and dry out the mud only to be joined again in further flurries and extremely bad weather? What I have stated to you over these last few pages and more is nothing compared to the real horrors of Passchendaele during this sodding war. The misery is simply too much to fathom; too much to sanely bear; it's impossible for you to completely understand unless you wear our boots and slog through the same mud that we have waded through.

20th NOVEMBER 1917

We were so decimated that the 8th and 9th Dublins were amalgamated and the 2nd were provided reinforcements to bring them back up to a reasonable strength. We were now prepared for the Battle of Cambrai and in particular, Tunnel Trench [which meant that we, the men of the 16th Irish Division, were to clear the way for the coming assaults upon the Hindenburg Line and beyond. The fact of the tale is that we were used as a diversionary almost eight miles away to the northwest from the centre of the main action. And let me tell you, we did not disappoint, for along with 3,000 yards of trench system captured we also took over 600 prisoners of war and 300 dead [this was an understatement of course and only those bodies of the enemy counted within the trenches themselves].

It was a reminder of the Battle of Langemarck with all the machinegun nests harboured in concrete surrounds; the only real difference was the way in which the trench system had been built with an underground tunnel in line with the front trench but 40 feet below it, staircases providing access to it every 25 yards. It was a marvel. These German engineers needed to be congratulated and I would have done so under different circumstances.

As a member of the 2nd Royal Dublin Fusiliers I was in the centre of the advance of our small portion of the attack and it smacked of the taste of normal Trench Warfare, but many circumstances placed much favour in our position.

There was some artillery at 0600hrs and we made good use of the stoke mortars in our sector. The stoke and its use of smoke proved to ruse the enemy into believing that they were being gassed and many, if not most, took to hiding below ground with their mask over their faces. At 0620hrs we left our line behind us and made our way forward.

The timing of the artillery was absolutely superb. We had 200 yards of no-man's land to cross and as we crossed this and fell upon the enemy; the artillery had been lifted from the area. It now came to the killing and what we could not see were dealt a savage hand as we cleared the tunnel system with bombs; there would be no counting the dead down there; not by me at least.

Sappers soon joined our victory and put to wiring up explosives to counter any enemy attack whilst the battle continues to rage in other areas around me. Some sectors encountered stiffer resistance than what I had encountered and for that I could only give praise, for I felt that I deserved just a small measure of relief.

With the fight still raging in places the main assault upon Cambrai was well on the way.

This would see the first real attempt at deploying tanks in large number and without the usual aid of a massive pre-planned artillery strike although the small barrage of just 1,003 guns at 0600hrs did well at their task of softening up the enemy positions. The lack of preliminary must have contributed to pulling the enemy off guard as did our diversionary attack for it all seemed to be met by a huge amount of success, which after the weeks now behind us was a welcome relief.

The amount of ground which we strove to win as an army was also granted in favour of our ambitious tactics and four miles was gained [five on the right flank] upon the newly fought ground known as the Hindenburg Line. It was so satisfying to be a part of something so memorable that I considered for just a moment that maybe I would get to see my loving family once more before I died. And is it not wondrous in years post how we remember the great days of war when amongst friends of old and then by night when sleep falls upon us we see the reality of it all as nightmares invade the security of our slumber? Yes; it's a jest.

But back to war I trudge in this short appraisal of my life on the front... yes; the church bells of Old England rang out the great victory for all to hear but it would be a short-lived celebration for the bastard sod had invented a new form of warfare and it involved twenty enemy divisions punching through to the rear of our line, bypassing the strong points, taking out our artillery and cutting off all resupply, creating a huge vacuum of confusion, and taking care of the pockets of resistance once a new front line had been established. Within a week all of our gains had been lost.

It was a dishonour to later learn that generals and the like were pushing and shoving to gain the praise for the initial victory of breaking through the Hindenburg Line where tanks and men fought side by side, but after the demise of the situation and our loss of ground there was not a hand to be seen anywhere. I despised them all for this, their clambering over each other for a good pat on the back but then failing to accept any responsibility; not for the loss of ground but for the loss of life itself. I was here to fight a war, not for the glory of a few head-strong generals.

But how did we fare; how was the battle waged; with artillery, smoke, 437 tanks and six infantry divisions. So can you do math? How many tanks to each battalion? [Approx 8 per battalion]. Well, I'm no good at math but I can tell you this; I saw bugger-all of any tanks but the occasional appearance of one to my farthest right flank, but then again the effects of war didn't allow me to think of this as a sight-seeing venture, in particular when your visions are marred by the dead and dying, and we were a part of the diversionary. And many mishaps as usual were encountered, like the attempt at capturing a bridge only to have it collapsed under the weight of the tanks as they endeavoured to cross it: when they built these bridges the thought of anything as heavy as a tank crossing over it would have been the furthest thing from the engineers' minds. 180 tanks were out of action that first day with 65 being utterly destroyed; there were in the vicinity of 71 mechanical failures and around 43 tanks which had been ditched, and I can only assume that some of these were those lost due to collapsing bridges.

It was said many times and recorded for prosperity that the diversion of the 16th was what provided the edge of victory whereby the first real signs of a true and possible end to the war could be seen; this, regardless of the losses to our gains.

By the end of it all what did we get? We received another transfer on the 3rd December to Gough's Fifth Army. I was a part of the 48th Brigade [1st and 2nd RDF with the 2nd Munster Fusiliers along for the ride].

DECEMBER 1917

Christmas Day: it's snowing hard as is to be expected. Maybe if we were pushing south instead of east the temperature would be friendlier towards our vocation and the lice less prone to bite, for the war always simmered during the colder months.

Try as I might I couldn't get comfortable enough to sleep even with my eyelids as heavy as heavy they were and although all logic told me to stay still and remain warm I was destined to relieve myself before what I carried in my bladder froze within me and made it impossible to do anything further.

I got up and commenced to make my way to a spot where I could do my duty without making our lives any more miserable by urinating where I stood. I hadn't gone far when I fell upon two men. One seemed to ignore the other for his antics were the strangest and most worrisome I had ever seen.

Give me my baby, he would say. Pass me my baby, I can't reach it. I would look and see that he was talking of a tin cup just out of reach of his extended fingers which bore the horrendous sign of frostbite. Give me my baby, he would say. And so I picked up the tin cup and gave it to him. He pulled it into his chest and hugged it, cradling it in his arms, smiling down upon the thing which if not used for drinking out of might be used for pissing into. There was no doubt in my mind that he was out of his and so I did the only thing possible; I ignored it. What should happen if I was to report him but a couple of MPs might appear with a bullet in the chamber? He seemed to have a friend sitting beside him and maybe it was his task to tend to his friend. I can only assume that when next we went over the top that he would still be their cradling his cup and some officer might fall upon him and take pity before the MPs caught sight of him.

Did I do my duty? Did I do what should have been done? I cannot carry the weight of the world upon my shoulders. There are many men around who, no doubt, knew him better than I. I should only hope that I did not come to form the same illusions upon my own mind.

And with the end of winter coming towards us we could feel the robustness of war falling back into place. Our numbers in February, due to many reasons as expressed these past four years, had dwindled at an alarming rate. We now received a...

143

refurbishment. The 8th, 9th, and 10th Dublin's were disbanded and with just under 200 men combined they were amalgamated into the 1st and 2nd Dublin's: we now had new stock but for the most part they were older hands as opposed to new; this literally meant better chances of survival for us all; unless we were to be thrown to the lions once more.

21st MARCH 1918

By 1918 we were inundated with warnings of gas attacks through the use of a bell system. It was a powerful air horn which had a good range of nine miles, but sometimes hard to hear between bouts of shelling, and most of us older men seemed to be growing rather deaf. We had also learnt to leave signs about warning others coming into the trenches that gas had been employed within the area or might be likely due to an expected up-and-coming sod attack; and the good word was that an attack was imminent.

It was during this month and commencing this day that many factor in the sods' disposition, both military and civilians alike, strove to make their mark upon the declining war effort. It was clear that the citizenry were appalled at the German losses as much so as they were starving to death: it would appear that they were growing as tired of the war as we were but they were the bastards that had started it. These face values of the effects of war came tumbling towards us in orders and the occasion newspaper that one man or other might be sent here and there, we were also provided information of the enemy disposition which did not look too grand.

There was an instance, or should I say, a terrible tragedy; the Russians surrendered and a treaty was signed, called the Treaty of Brest Litovsk; the sod was therefore able to move, as fast as they could possibly muster, 50 divisions towards the BEF and the soon-to-arrive Yanks. It was said, and I quite believe it [though I'm sure the generalship would rather have these figures understated to prevent panic] that there were around 184, give or take, sodding divisions in France and Flanders, 241 divisions when accounting for all: 110 divisions on the front line and 31 divisions facing the BEF with more than 60 in reserve. With the Americans arriving at our backs sooner rather than later it was time for the Germans to push and push hard before our friends at our back could establish themselves and form upon our flanks and possibly even amongst us.

I should, I think, give you an estimate. A German division now averaged 12,300 men; due to losses and restructure our divisions comprised approximately 4,500. The sodding division was also well afforded 3,000 horses, 48 guns, 120 mortars, 78 HMG, 144 LMG and a dozen trucks. With all of this upon my mind I could clearly see that they were to either throw everything they had at us or stand and fight in a last-ditch effort to wipe us clean from the face of the earth, for there could be no other explanation for such a well-fitted organisation when the countries populace was so ill-at-ease.

There is but one last thing which I think I should mention and that is of the sods' newly invented weapon-of-war. They had invented a form of soldier called the stormtrooper, the cream of all other divisions, the fittest and best taken from here and there to form divisions of fearsome men who would be cut at the leash to advance upon and through us, cutting off and destroying all communication, artillery, headquarters, support, resupply, and so on and so forth. They had used them against the Russians and now it was to be our turn.

The lead up to this days hard duty were masked with gas attacks to keep us from sleep and they did their work well for I was beginning to forget how long it had been since I had good slumber, but my mind perks up during the opening of the artillery and even more so when I see for the first time the flammerwerfen coming towards me, those evil men with flame-throwers with jets of flame spurting thirty yards out from the nozzle. The prettiest sight is seeing them flicker and die as they run out of fuel but it's a seldom thing to witness, and it is the last thing you wish to think about as you scramble to kill the men who employ them or try to seek cover as men burn around you, and you know you have to pray to God once more on conceding that you must now regain his trust after years of neglect and cold-shoulder.

When there is a wall of flame approaching you, you must gather all you can on your side and I apologize to you if you think I am using God to save my life before deciding to shun him again once more, but since those heinous days of morbid horror I have stayed by his side in belief even if not being as attentive in practise.

We had already [the 1st and 2nd Dublins] suffered extremely heavy casualties from the initial bombardment and the sods use of poison gas [1,062 casualties from both combined] and so it was easy, with all that was happening, for the German forces of new to spill over us and keep on moving: do I need to remind you that the normal strength for a battalion was 1,000 men but for some time now many battalions were operating with as few as 500 due to losses; can you see now how so many casualties over a short period of ten hours, even before the whistle blew for the sodding infantry to fall upon us, would see the bastards gain so much ground by penetrating our lines of defence? 1,100,000 artillery shells in five hours they fired over an area of just 150 square miles. That was horrendous, the largest bombardment of the war. And now more of the same slaughter to come. It was here that those Germans bringing up the rear would take-care of those men caught behind by any means they could, to clean our small pockets of resistance up as best they could; I can only thank God that what was left of the 2nd were able to retreat as ordered. Many men along the front were taken prisoner but being taken alive was better than burning to death. As for me and many around we were lucky to escape with our lives, to live and continue fighting as we evacuated our positions.

The sheer horror of those days is not to be contemplated lightly. In three days we had lost all the gains we'd made since Passchendaele. The enemy were pushing as hard as they could and their new front line left behind them hundreds upon hundreds of pockets of resistance and we continued to fight as best we could. Those men left behind had no food, were low on ammo, and had no communications and little to no support. All any of us could do was to hold out as best we could whether on the move towards the west or holding out in pockets. The worst of the enemy action was by no means over but for some the main assault had come and gone, and they were now targeting those of the mopping up operations. Many men fought to the last, refusing to surrender and hence giving their life to duty and their country. My only hope during those dark days was that we could hold out long enough for our good men to form up and strike back; my hope was that we could continue our retreat in reasonable good order and not get caught out like so many that had been left behind.

22nd MARCH 1918

It was seen as a gift that those left behind were still fighting and delaying the enemy advance. This was the second day of Operation Michael, the second day of the sodding offensive. It reminded me a little of the retreat from Mons for we were mobile. Trench Warfare seems to have faded away into oblivion.

We retreated; the engineers blew up bridges; the sod did all they could to keep the gap between us closed. But they seemed so disordered and acted erratically. The disorder could not last for long, surely, but then again I guess it was all about who could outlast the disorder the longest for we were not in any great state ourselves. Men from difficult units were fighting with others, here and there it seemed to be the accepted way of today's war to fight with men from units that you didn't know. It was up to the officers and NCOs to take command of what they could and retain some form of discipline, but discipline was never our problem; our issues were always the generals and out-dated policies.

In some places the retreat was holding its own, in others the enemy had penetrated more than ten miles with pockets of resistance being looked to by the enemy reserve. It was not an easy picture to decipher, let alone paint.

25th MARCH 1918

Some good news; the enemy seems to have advanced as far as they can manage. They were as exhausted as us, if not more; their artillery and resupply could not keep up the pace as was similar to four years previous during Mons: they had not learnt their lessons well. The 16th Irish have also been transferred back to the Third Army.

We were suffering from a lack of food but the enemy were suffering from a lack of artillery. It was a bitter-sweet period of the war, but I guess it is best to be alive and hungry than ducking your head before it gets blown away from shelling.

There was a moments peace in the air, a little solace to tend our minds, and then the enemy seemed to suddenly pick themselves up and continue on, the pace quickened once more, the hectic war continuing on for God knows how many days to come. Again we were moving alongside civilians with their carts and wagons stacked high with all manner of possession, moving at best speed away from the stormtroopers, flammerwerfen and death. The cavalry, also, did their bit as before, their actions being the toast of the day.

26th MARCH 1918

The stage was set for the Doullens conference and the newest tank from England, the Whippet, was to make its debut, a tank that was lighter and faster than the Mark IV. The enemy, in large number, fled the advance of twelve of these. A small dominoes effect then saw to it that other German infantry were left without support and consequently taken by force, for the remainder of the day new lines were drawn upon the map and the force from both sides found their footing upon the ground in most sectors.

Disposition? Names like the River Somme, Albert, and Ancre all came back into use; names of places where we'd bled over the years. The ground lost was an enormous blow to morale but we managed to keep our heads above water. Four days later on the

30th we were subjugated to the last real German attack. It was near the Somme. We gave a little ground and they gave a lot of blood; ground for blood; I think we achieved the better deal and so with a smile upon my face I try my best to grasp some sleep, but sleep wouldn't come too easily. The 16th Irish was down to a single infantry battalion and I was still alive. Should I feel some small portion of guilt for being alive when so many were dead? How many had suffered and lost their life? How many Old Sweats were there left remaining? How many men that I had joined with were there still alive today? I should think that the answer was not worth knowing for it would only demoralise me further and it was hard enough to maintain a reasonably healthy mind as it was.

And what will tomorrow bring?

31st MARCH 1918

Shall I give it to you in detail or shall I just give it? You have read so much of me and the war and I should hope that you grow tired of hearing about the death and bloody carnage. If you are one that wants to hear more than maybe you are a bloodsucker; I can't help it; that's what you are, reading this miserable peace of crap for your own desire... I'm sorry... forgive me. It is only a few days from today that the 1st and 2nd Royal Dublin Fusiliers were amalgamated. Alongside us are the 5th Royal Irish Fusiliers, 500 Americans and 400 Canadians. What did we do...? We have stopped the German advance near Hamel; we marked the end of the war. We had done it. We had kicked the bastard so hard that he was bleeding from the nose and cowering. The French were on their feet, the Yanks [God bless those bastards] have arrived in number and such resupply. The Germans had failed to separate the allies by force, had failed to push us into the sea. It was time for us to commence our hitting and not to let go until we had won the war.

The Germans launch smaller attacks here and there and are largely unsuccessful.

And so the war trudges along and is all more of the same but we feel as though we are on the front foot and mostly eager to get it over with. By June some of our men have gone to the 1st and we are left with a skeleton crew of battle-hardened veterans; we are also so few that we are transferred temporarily to the Lines of Communication [LOC]. So here we are, running here and there, passing along orders, helping with resupply, and giving aid to communications in general.

APRIL 1918

I think it's time to see the light at the end of the tunnel. The heading of my story has been well explained and it is during the month of April that the Virgin Mary was to fall. It's felling is also obscured from truth for there is one claim that British Artillery knocked her down from her perch and yet another from a German officer. I tend to think it was the Germans and this is how they went about it.

During their last efforts to hold onto Alfred, having gained her once more during the previous month, it was time to take it back which we did with great honour. The tower once again could be employed to great advantage by using it as a spotting tower for bringing artillery to bear upon the enemy as well as a machine gun being in place and employed to carve up the sod quite nicely. It is here that a German Army Order is received by the 5th Corps Heavy Artillery that no more buildings were to be demolished by fire, an instant later and another officer, Colonel in rank, makes contact with the fifth and requested artillery fire upon the tower due to the allied machine gun being in place.

A young German captain of the times answers the call for aid. Seeing that he is in a position to calculate and give an order he readies himself for an exercise with great initiative. He cannot directly break the original Army Order but can place artillery fire to bear upon enemy positions. The young captain plots his coordinates to destroy an imagined trench line of enemy and orders a battery to fire upon it. He knows full well that the

150

trajectory itself will fall upon the tower and it isn't long before his calculations bear fruit. The Virgin Mary is no more.

However, there is a small flaw with this for it is also said that what remained of the Virgin Mary when she fell was carried away by the Germans and melted down as scrap. If this is true then it surely must have been the British artillery that had knocked her down for only if the Germans were in possession of the tower and in place upon the ground, with time up their sleeve, could they have carried the statue away.

This is simply another one of these stories similar to the Angels of Mons which will tear us apart. It's sometimes hard to believe what you read and so I tend to trust my own eyes rather than the stories posed by others.

1st JUNE 1918

We were no longer a part of the LOC but now in the 31st Division as a training cadre. I do believe that these past couple of months have been a reward for our overwhelming losses these past few years; which I accept. But this wasn't to last long.

6th June – we were reconstituted and brought it men from the 7th Battalion.

16th June – we were transferred to the 50th Northumbrian Division.

28th September – we were preparing for our counter-offensive to take back all we had lost and more some. We were the 1st, 2nd, and 7th Dublins.

29th SEPTEMBER 1918

This was the Battle of St Quentin Canal and a most deciding factor for the sodding bastards to see the defeat of their strengths written upon the wall for all time. British, American, Australian; we were here under the command of… an Australian, and we coherently achieved all of our objectives and smashed through that impenetrable system of bunkers which was the Siegfried and Hindenburg lines.

It wasn't just the metal of the men that achieved this wonderful success but the metal of the tanks intertwined with us, the Americans taking the lead and the units behind using the leap-frog method of movement to continue an arduous pace towards the enemy positions and machinegun bunkers.

Without the American support I doubt that we would have achieved success so thoroughly and as quickly but success would have been achieved in the long run. It was to be expected, regardless of this support, that the Americans were not quite up to the war for their training was slightly inadequate, but the resources were a glorious thing. As our leap-frog move forward came into effect the Australians found many pockets of Americans sticking hard to the ground without leadership but they soon tagged along with the Australians and fought side-by-side.

Yes indeed, name calling and all jokes aside the men of all calibre and nationality gave aid to one another as though born of the same family, heritage and blood. We strove to make the sod pay for all they had done these past four years and pay dearly they did.

Prisoners were taken much more easily now than ever before. They knew that they had lost the war and were happy to see and easy way to get through it with their lives intact. We were much the same in that contrast, each and every one of us, regardless of which side we fought on, wanted nothing more than to spend the rest of our lives at peace and with loved ones. And I was shocked to hear from the mouth of one prisoner what the officers were telling them, as they fired their weapons through the mouth of bunkers and over the lip of trenches, that it was the civilians back home in Germany that had lost the war, not the soldiers. The slide remarks must have been meant; a true-to-the-heart comment felt by many, for it was no good trying to stoke the morale of soldiers any longer for officers must surely have seen that the fight was falling from them on a daily basis.

You may think that I have left out the Canadians; not by any means. By the 8th October they came together and poured all they had into the Battle of Cambrai, a super-fast storming and bombardment of infantry supported by 324 tanks, the defenders overwhelmed so quickly and so decisively. The Canadian casualties were light.

And now I must speak of something that I did experience and that is the Battle of Courtrai, also known as the Second Battle of Belgium.

OCTOBER 1918

The Battle of Courtrai was carried out in late September to early October and with the ease of things occurring the past weeks it was an understatement to realise that morale was peaking at its highest since the beginning of the war. The pictures were being painted for us all to see, the glory of the days ahead where we were the victors, the upholders of good against evil, for we were not the ones to have started this mess but surely here to clean it up.

We were to hit and hit hard, to keep the sods running until winter was truly upon us so that it was too cold for the sod to do anything to us in return but gain shelter in pits of mud; but with the many villages and such around it was hard to see how some little comfort could not be attained by us from time to time.

The Germans were retiring once more and so it was relatively easy to move into the town of Courtrai. The people of the town were so overjoyed by our arrival that it was as though we were stepping off a train in the heart of London itself to be delivered into the arms of the thankful. There before us all are 40,000 men, women, and children all clambering to get a clear view of us, to clasp our hands on this victorious day. They had been liberated and they knew it. The Germans had been the torturers and rulers for four long years and now they were free. None of them seemed to even consider that the sod might be back to lash out more of the same in the near future for it was more than adamantly clear that the war was near its end and that the allies were the victor. So happy they were that they flew their flags freely from atop churches, public buildings, and every window possible. Wherever you cared to look you could see the picture of their beloved Belgium King and Queen. They were beyond joyous rebellion, there were ecstatic for the freedom being handed them, a free gift for all they had suffered and had done. If this was how the war was to end then I did not mind as much as I had over the years past. The joy seen in the eyes of the young and old was so… I was almost on the verge of crying.

I can see past the crowd to a place where there are horses standing amongst a mass of people. The horses suddenly fall, having been slaughtered then and there. The people move in a cut away the flesh of one, for it to be cooked and eaten. So hungry they were; only then did I realize how truly, poorly these people had been treated, but worse was to come, naturally, for where there had been German soldiers then there had been misery and shocking displays of torture and rape such as a small boy with no fingers for they had been shot off one by one so that his mother would get on her back for the joy of half a dozen German men.

There was no other livestock in this town of 40,000, for every cow, hen and other form of life has been taken by the sod. Oh; it is also Sunday.

And when it is time to move on from the town we do so with the thousands waving us goodbye and into unknown territory we continue on, into country which we have never seen before, and it is wonderful. There are trees and grass like I have never seen in my entire life. It is like a scene from heaven. I cannot believe that there could be so many colours in life. It is so beautiful that the memories I have of home come suddenly flooding back and I can recall the fields and valleys of home. I am truly ready to get away from here and see my family once more.

16th OCTOBER 1918

You have heard me say 'the last offensive', or 'the last major battle' or words to this effect. For their size and complexity they were but there was one more that stood before us, for those men of the 2nd.

It was as though we could not be rewarded with a victory, nor a ticket home, until our unit had been culled once more and so we met this day with trepid anxiety.

I am not going to go into details for it is much of the same. It is more killing and bloodshed as ever I saw, but not nearly as bad as the Somme and the few other battles that stacked the mounting dead beside it. But what I shall tell you will make you think like I: how the hell did I survive the war? We suffered 44 per cent casualties within just two days; this was the end of the war for me and the others of our unit, a unit which had been present from the very beginning, having arrived on the soil at the commencement of hostilities. And although it was the last time I should see conflict, other than the rare glimpse or odd shot now and again, the same can't be said for the 1st Royal Dublin Fusiliers who fought heroically as ever at the Battle of the Sambre on the 4th day of November, 1918.

We were now advancing a good five miles a day and this continued until the following week.

11th NOVEMBER 1918

The war is ended.

It is cold and there is a heavy frost. I can still hear firing but only a trickle compared to the past.

The Armistice was signed early on the morning of this day but wasn't to come into effect until 1100hrs. Further to this the soldiers on both sides of the fence, so to speak, weren't told of this until the actual day. I have no real understanding why this might have been other than to consider that the generals in command of us might of seen a tendency for soldiers to act too peacefully and hence place the front line in jeopardy should things go astray. As it were they had nothing to worry about for the fighting continued here and there right up until the eleventh hour.

As for my dear wife at home she wasn't to hear the news until 1020hrs, when David George made the announcement over the radio for all to hear.

Shelling continued on the line and around 11,000 casualties were suffered, more than 2,700 dying of their wounds, either instantaneously or in great pain. It is a terrible waste of life as it is but to die on the last day when you know the war to be over is sheer agony.

I have heard in recent years that the last man to die of the allies was an American named Henry Gunther, being stupid and beyond compare by charging a small group of Germans and being shot. What manner of thought goes through a man's head at such a time? As for the Germans it was after 1100hrs that a death was recorded; being an officer of lower rank he decided to approach a small group of Americans to advise them that he was handing over the houses that his men had been using, so that they themselves could harbour there. The Americans shot him and their excuse was that they did not know the war was over.

We celebrated as would be expected, smiles all around being shared, for it was almost time to go home. We were soon quietened down and advised that we had a hefty walk ahead of us to get to the nearest point of departure, but before that we needed to gather some supplies and have ourselves a smoke.

Our officers also did a tour of the ranks to try and get us to sign on for another 12 months. They needed soldiers to stay behind, to clean up the battlefield, to put the dead to rest and help bring a little order back to the country so devastated by war. I for one was to refuse. I had been here more than four years and had earned my ticket home. Surely the men who'd recently arrived should volunteer, those men who had only been here a month or more, maybe a year or two; get them to stay behind. And so I stood in line and waited for my demobilisation papers on reaching a bivouac of necessity. Again I was asked, most formally, to sign on for an extended stay but all I could manage was a smile and a no thank you. I was looking forward to being home with family and friends but didn't know how many friends had survived the war, but on return I found it hard to return to civilian life and harder to accept that there were able-bodied men here that had refused to fight and instead remained behind making ten, no, a hundred times more than I was making as I fought both tooth and nail to stay alive. I was utterly disgusted by these men.

And shall I tell you of my first embrace with my family, of how happy I was and they were? Do I really need to? I think not.

HISTORICAL NOTE

As the writer of this text, which I consider to be historical-fiction more so than a true event for the simple reason that I cannot guarantee in any way that dates, formations, or locations, are precise, I must apologise if I have got-it-wrong.

For all intents and purposes the research I have conducted points to a narrative that is true in every word apart from the fact that the 2nd Royal Dublin Fusiliers may not have been at Ypres on 22nd October 1914 [as an example] but to otherwise give you, the reader, a more precise understanding of the war it has been required of me to see that my Great Grandfather was 'here' or 'there' in order to give clarity and light to 'this' and 'that' situation.

You might ask yourself what right do I have to play with his thoughts as I have done; what experience have I had which might allow me to say what I have said. I was in Rwanda, 1995; in country at the time of the Kibeho Massacre which saw 10,000 killed for no good reason other than racial vilification; I was here during the build-up of hostilities between the 18th to 21st of April, the general massacre occurring on 22nd April; I further experienced what many others in UNAMIR II did experience during the day afterwards, endeavouring to see the survivors given aid and moved on to their home communes from the 23rd of that month to the 9th May, 1995.

I should also like to state that my Grandfather was one of the first to enter Bergen Belsen during WWII and he saw the atrocities of that camp for himself. He was initially in the infantry, the Royal West Kent, but later transferred to MPs.

And so with such a family-orientated, military background, and much research conducted on Kibeho, Bergen-Belsen, and WWI, I see this text as written history, regardless of whether the man I have placed on the ground, and spoken for him on his behalf, may or may not have been at a particular post at a particular time.

I have done all I could to ensure he was in certain areas during particular battles and hope that you don't remember this book for what he has done and where, but to remember this story in the memory of all those that fought during it and then have to face further troubles when arriving home, to find themselves without work and practically forgotten.

My Great, Grandfather's first two children were born in Ireland and I believe they came to England during the Easter Sunday Massacre but I'm not 100% on this. Blighty for him would have been a headache, for travel time, to and fro, is part-n-parcel of the leave itself. Someone living in Kent would see their son, father, husband, for a good 10 days out of 14; for someone living in Ireland it would reduce his leave significantly, to the point of being pointless. Whether or not my Great Grandfather's wife and first son would have made an effort to get to England would have been doubtful, in particular during the time when he was injured. As to whether or not he received any other injury I do not know, but it would be hard to believe that he escaped with nothing else but the agony of being gassed. I cannot say whether or not he was promoted but given the circumstances of his being alive for the entirety of the war it is hard to believe that he wouldn't have at least made the rank of sergeant.

Thank you for reading.